How to
Understand and
Influence People
and Organizations

How to
Understand and
Influence People
and Organizations

*Practical Psychology for
Goal Achievement*

Michael R. Perlson

amacom
A DIVISION OF AMERICAN MANAGEMENT ASSOCIATIONS

158.7
P42

88979

Library of Congress Cataloging in Publication Data

Perlson, Michael R.
  How to understand and influence people and organizations.

  Includes index.
  1. Psychology, Industrial.   2. Organizational behavior.
I. Title.
HF5548.8.P399   158.7   81-69357
ISBN 0-8144-5684-7   AACR2

First Printing

To my father, Norman Perlson, who taught me the joy of games. To my mother, Lilyan Perlson, who taught me with love. To my wife, Randy Perlson, who taught me love without games. To my friend Stan Acker, who taught me to pay attention to the rules of the game; and to my partner, Mark Lewin, who taught me how to play games well. Last but not least, to my children—Aaron, Rachel, and Joshua—who find my games silly but who love me anyway.

Preface

The game of management is a difficult one. It requires luck, skill, and a touch of magic. Goals and objectives are like glass targets. They glitter and twinkle in the corporate sunlight—some clear, some frosted, and still others highly mirrored: what you see is not always what you hit.

I have chosen the word "game" because it fits for me. I am indebted to an old TV show called *Beat the Clock* for the idea. A contestant is given a simple task such as trundling back and forth between a tub and a bucket, filling one with water from the other. At the last instant before the game starts, a few "rules" are added. Such rules include wearing lead tennis shoes and being blindfolded. As with any game, you have to know the rules. It also helps if you have a sense of humor.

This is a book for and about managers. It is based on my training as a psychologist and my experience as an organization consultant. There is a gaping hole between the two that needs to be filled. I offer no new organization theories or management gimmicks, only what I hope is a clear concise guide to what is useful and practical in the behavioral sciences. That such a need exists is exemplified by the office of my very first client. Resting on his highly polished credenza was about a yard of management books. From Argyris to Zalkind, he had them all. "A very impressive collection," I offered. "Oh, they just came with the office," he replied.

If you bought this book for decoration, I have a suggestion. Remove the cover and give the rest to a friend. Wrap the cover around a piece of wood of appropriate size. Indeed, that's what this book is all about—making the maximum use of available resources. Management is a game of hitting targets. Just to make it interesting, they are made of glass. Thus, most of what you see is distorted.

Consider this book a pair of funny glasses that will enable you to see people, groups, and organizations from a new perspective. Not that you are blind or I am so keen-sighted, but I suspect that you may be a little light on depth perception. I have learned a lot from you, and this is my chance to return the favor.

One final *caveat:* the names of most of the organizations I will discuss have been changed to protect the innocent, the guilty, and—most of all—me. Any similarity between these names and real ones is unintentional, but the cases themselves are quite true.

MICHAEL R. PERLSON

Contents

PART I
PEOPLE

O wad some power the giftie gie us,
to see oursel's as others see us!

Famous speech therapist

1

Individual Behavior

I sees the enemy and they is us.

Famous possum

People do not behave logically, they behave psychologically. This is unfair, unjust, and very inconvenient. Nevertheless, it's true. Understanding why people do what they do is as absolutely essential to the game of management as knowing the laws of probability is to poker. Such knowledge will not guarantee that you will win the game, but ignorance will condemn you to a life of drawing to inside straights.

The fundamentals of human behavior can be written neatly on a postcard. But, since a postcard carries neither the prestige nor the income of a textbook, most authors flesh out a few rather simple rules into a prodigious tome that tries to make up in bulk what it lacks in clarity. When you boil away the fat and water, you end up with Rule 1.

> *Rule 1:* People always act in their own best interest,
> given the facts as they know them.

When we see people spending a significant portion of each day walking in tight circles, we tend to label them "crazy" and often institutionalize them. What the casual observer fails to note, though, is that in terms of their perception and experience, circling is the very best solution they have to cope with life.

All theories of behavior are variations on the theme of the first phrase in Rule 1. The key, however, is in the last phrase: *given the facts as they know them*. Since no two people ever see the world in exactly the same way, there is an infinite set of "facts." Thus, the secret to understanding human behavior is to see the world as others see it—which, of course, is easier said than done.

Motivation

What a lovely word; it literally rolls off your tongue. Although originally buried in scholarly works, it has become a popular buzzword in discussions of human behavior. In its most basic form, the concept of motivation is defined by Rule 2.

Rule 2: People act to meet needs.

Abraham Maslow, a psychologist, expanded this principle into a hierarchy of needs. He argued that when a lower-level need is satisfied, the person is no longer motivated by it and advances to the next plateau. Although it sounds like a TV game show, the notion is simple and sound. In descending order, the five levels of needs in Maslow's hierarchy are:

1. self-actualization
2. self-esteem
3. social needs (love and belonging)
4. security
5. physiological needs

Maslow's mistake was in assuming that people are rational organisms who share the same "facts." At the bottom rung, you are unlikely to get a teenager and a nutritionist to agree on what constitutes necessary food. In the stratosphere of self-actualization, where people are urged to pull their own strings, win through intimidation, and paddle their own canoe, it is very hard to agree on what epitomizes such behavior. Indeed, there is a strong argument that "typical" behavior does not exist. Since self-actualization is making the best possible use of what you've got, it is either true for all of us ("That really is the best I can do."), or none of us ("There is always room for improvement."). Such ambiguity calls for a revision of Rule 2.

Rule 2: People act to meet *perceived* needs.

Now you can understand why my physiological needs will not be met by cauliflower, regardless of how well cooked. All parents—and some managers—know that there is a significant difference between needs and wants. Wants are what our charges say *they* need: needs are what we know *we* want. Most interpersonal conflict is reflected in the lament: "Why don't they want what I want them to want?"

Physiological Needs

People live in their bodies. Bodies need air, water, food, and sleep to stay alive. Those whose basic needs are only marginally met often suffer emotionally and intellectually. Their struggle for survival becomes all-consuming, with little energy left to meet higher-level needs.

There is a saying that every country is but three meals away from a revolution. In our high-technology society, we sometimes forget how tenuously our basic needs are protected. Only in times of disaster are most Americans really likely to get in touch with their physiological needs; the threat to survival is no longer of practical concern in motivating people to work in America. Minimum wage laws, unemployment compensation, and public assistance provide reasonable defense against starvation. Gone are the breadlines of the Great Depression.

But other societies are different. For example, when a large fruit company first began to harvest crops in the Pacific, there was great difficulty with the native laborers. Once they earned enough to purchase sufficient food for themselves and their families, the natives did not return to work until their stores were depleted. The company's solution, albeit a manipulative one, was to provide each spouse with a Sears Roebuck catalog. The result was a significant reduction in absenteeism. Wages were, for the first time, perceived as more than food. Huts were filled with blankets, washers, and the myriad "needs" that previously were not wanted.

To paraphrase Maslow, man does not live by bread alone—unless there is no bread. When his belly is regularly filled, other needs emerge; the psychological hungers then take over.

The Psychological Hungers

Unlike water and food, security is both a physical and a psychological experience. It involves emotional safety as well as protection from harm. The key element is fear. That some people continue to feel "scared to death" suggests that their perceived need for security remains unsatisfied.

In spite of the demonstrably paralyzing effects of feeling scared, some managers still cling to the myth of motivation by fear. Indeed, for those employees who already carry a heavy load of insecurity, the mere raising of an eyebrow can set them to trembling.

A more subtle corollary to this approach is the concept of positive reward, commonly applied in the form of pay incentives, promotions, and other organizational payoffs. It was Frederick Herzberg who first pointed out that neither the "push" of punishment nor the "pull" of reward is an example of motivation. He likens the former to rape and the latter to seduction. In either case the individual has little real choice.

Herzberg's major contribution was to demonstrate that job satisfaction and dissatisfaction were *not* opposites. This confounding bit of semantics is based on the notion that people behave psychologically, not logically.

In a neat bit of enfolding, Herzberg collapsed Maslow's hierarchy into two sets of needs. One set involves the basic biological needs and the built-in drive to avoid pain. The other set relates to the ability to achieve and, through achievement, to experience psychological growth. Only in the latter case does the meeting of a need reflect the process of motivation. The clue was a four-letter word in Maslow's triangle—*self*. In the pursuit of esteem and self-actualization, the individual alone is responsible. He or she can be neither manipulated, raped, nor seduced.

The Need for Achievement

A well-read business executive once exclaimed, "I am perched atop Maslow's hierarchy and it hurts like hell!" The work of psychologist David C. McClelland has greatly focused on the *need for achievement*, defined as the need for success in relation to an internalized standard of excellence. His conclusions to date have been that behavior associated with this need occurs only in a minority of the population, but it can be taught. Such behavior reflects concern with personal achievement rather than with the rewards of success. It is a subtle but important difference.

A most critical component to the definition of the need for achievement is "internalized standard of excellence." One price we have paid for the Industrial Revolution has been the slow disappearance of the craftsman. To achieve such status one had to produce a masterpiece, a tangible *external* standard of excellence. You could see it, hold it, and feel its shape and texture. Today's worker has no such luxury. He or she must look *inside* to determine excellence. And as McClelland has demonstrated, very few are motivated to look.

Because the need for achievement deals only with a minor part of behavior, McClelland developed two additional concepts: the *need for power*, defined as the need to control or influence others, and the *need for affiliation*, defined as the need for close interpersonal relationships and friendships.

The needs for achievement, power, and affiliation, can be demonstrated in groups performing tasks. In the first case people act to set moderate but achievable goals. When power needs predominate, the people seem most concerned with authority and who's in charge. In the third case they place greater importance on who they work with. All are important distinctions when assigning activities to groups.

The contrast between the two approaches to needs and motivation is striking. Maslow focuses on generalized human behavior, while McClelland hones in on individual differences. Taking them together, we can create a pyramid of motivation that summarizes what we know about why people act. This model is illustrated in Figure 1.

Faced with the need for physical survival, it is unlikely that people will quibble over job descriptions, shift differentials, or coffee breaks. Once basic needs are met, however, individual differences become a major factor. For example, some hourly workers see overtime as a reward, and others view it as a punishment.

Reward and Punishment

Since the days of Pavlov and his drooling dogs, there has been a great deal of misunderstanding about how reward and punishment affect behavior. The facts are:

1. What meets a need is a reward; it generates more of the same behavior.
2. What blocks a need is punishment; it generates avoidance behavior.

On the surface, a person's responses to reward and punishment appear to be the same. But they are very different. This difference is central to understanding human behavior.

A reward is a reward only if it meets a need, which is why a child may discard an expensive toy to play with the box it came in. It is also why employee "gifts" will displease as many as they delight.

Figure 1. The pyramid of motivation.

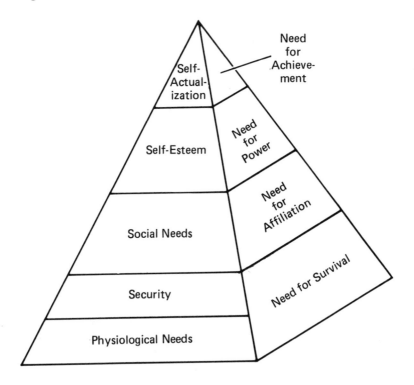

The probability of a large group sharing the same need is astronomically low.

Punishment or the threat of punishment *seems* to prevent behaviors associated with it. In reality, though, it merely encourages people to avoid the punishment—in other words, to try not to get caught. In this context it is easy to see that the natural response to radar-enforced speed control is a "fuzz buster." This is also why most employees take all their paid sick leave as extra vacation time in spite of management's lament that they should only take sick leave when genuinely ill.

All these points can be summarized as Rule 3.

> *Rule 3:* People meet needs by getting rewards and
> avoiding punishment.

Conclusions

Managers have been wrestling for decades with the thorny issue of why people act as they do. The result has been a wide range of programs from incentives and job enrichment to behavior modification. Each has had only limited success, and none has been a great golden cure-all.

Organizations are not designed to meet the needs of people. Factories and offices are built to perform tasks. The modern assembly line is a marvel of technology, but it is a wasteland in terms of opportunity to meet needs for achievement, power, or even affiliation.

This is the hard reality of the work environment. Most attempts to improve productivity through increasing employee satisfaction have failed miserably. The major components of workflow are determined by economic considerations. Very little can be modified to meet individual needs, particularly when they differ from person to person.

An answer, then, is to put the shoe on the other foot: individuals must take responsibility for evaluating their own needs and matching them to the characteristics of the job. In this way, the manager can assume the role of counselor rather than of judge and jury.

This is not to say that organizations can do nothing to improve the situation. Rather, their efforts to meet employee needs must focus on individual differences, not on broad generalizations. Such constructive approaches include "flex-time," variable compensation packages, and consideration of work-area design. It is, after all, the psychological considerations, not the technical components of a job, that will determine the level of worker motivation. Even then, the impact on productivity will be marginal.

A case in point is the "Hawthorne effect." Some 50 years ago a study was conducted at the Hawthorne, Illinois, Western Electric plant. Employees were removed to a special room in which physical conditions were periodically altered. Whatever changes were made—even when illumination and rest conditions were poor—

productivity increased. For years, this experiment was cited as "proof" that special attention to affiliative needs would increase performance, regardless of actual working conditions.

Recently, a reexamination of this study revealed two factors not mentioned by the original experimenter. First, employees were given regular feedback on how productive they were; second, they were paid well above those not participating in the study. Thus many different needs were met.

In conclusion, the three basic rules of human behavior are:

Rule 1: People always act in their own best interest,
given the facts as they know them.
Rule 2: People act to meet perceived needs.
Rule 3: People meet needs by getting rewards and
avoiding punishment.

Taken together, these rules can help managers hit real targets rather than shadows or reflections. In subsequent chapters they will be applied to real work situations and common management problems.

References

Hertzberg, Frederick (with Bernard Mausner and Barbara B. Snyderman), *The Motivation to Work*. New York: John Wiley, 1959.

James, Muriel (with Louis Savary), *The Heart of Friendship*. San Francisco: Harper & Row, 1976.

Maslow, Abraham H., "A Theory of Human Motivation." *Psychological Review*, July 1943.

McClelland, David C., "That Urge to Achieve." *Think Magazine*, I.B.M., 1966.

2

Group Behavior

There is strength in numbers.

Famous accountant

When John took a new job, he was excited about his prospects. He hoped to put all of his training and experience together with ideas he wanted to share with the group. It didn't take long for him to learn that people didn't seem to want his new ideas. After six months, John was convinced that the only people who got ahead were those who kept their mouths shut and did what they were told. Meetings were pleasant and everyone went along with the boss's recommendations.

People seemed to like their jobs and the company. Most of them had been around a long time. John's attempts to raise questions and make suggestions were met with an indulgent smile from his boss, who told him to "keep up the good work." As for his ideas, nothing more was heard about them.

John sensed something was wrong, but he could not put his finger on anything concrete. People treated him well, work went smoothly, and the future seemed secure. Yet there was pressure from his group to "sit tight" and not make waves, and John knew he wanted more out of his work, more challenge and stimulation, a chance to have a real impact. He began to wonder if he had made a mistake in taking this job.

Groups are a natural phenomenon in organizations. Most large organizations are composed of a large number of groups that interact, negotiate, compete, cooperate, and form coalitions. For management, groups can be a means of controlling individual behavior. For individuals, groups can serve as a way to achieve power. Between management and individuals, a great deal of energy is generated. Alas, too often more of this energy is dissipated than is put to productive use. Indeed, just as organizations have been designed to accomplish tasks rather than meet individual needs, so it is true that *formal* organizational structure rarely reflects how work groups function in fact. To begin at the beginning, let's look at the dynamics of group behavior.

Group Dynamics

A group is a collection of people who exhibit stable and *predictable* interaction. It is defined in terms of space, time, and behavior. A bunch of folks riding in an elevator are certainly physically close, but they are not a group. Passengers who travel regularly on the same commuter train may spend considerable time together, but they are not a group. Car pools, on the other hand, are often groups. The key element is one of relationship—more specifically, of cohesiveness. In groups, cohesion is most often a function of dependency: the more an individual's needs are met by a group, the greater the dependency and thus the higher the cohesiveness. In the first two examples, there is no such dependency because trains and elevators will run regardless of the other passengers' presence.

The development of cohesion and the functioning of a group are illustrated in Figure 2.

An individual attempts to join a group in order to meet certain perceived needs. If these needs are met, a dependency relationship forms, assuming, of course, that the individual meets the group's requirements for membership. As dependency among group members grows, cohesion increases. If needs are not met, as in John's case, withdrawal—either physical or emotional—will result. On the other hand, if membership requirements are not met (such as not making waves), expulsion will result.

All of the above applies to the formation and development of

Figure 2. **Group formation.**

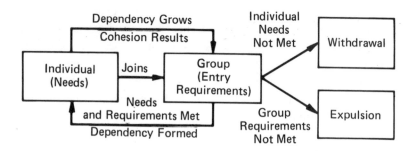

"informal" groups, which are the natural result of people sharing time, space, and dependency. The typical work group, however, is not a natural formation, but rather a number of individuals pressed into an already existing structure by outside forces. The net result is two pictures of the group: the formal structure (how management thinks it is) and the informal structure (how it really is). The dissonance between these two views provides the basis for much misunderstanding about what goes on in work groups.

The Words and the Music

The interaction of people in work groups can be observed at two levels: *content,* which describes the specific tasks or problems being dealt with, and *process,* which focuses on *how* such issues are dealt with. Together they provide the words and the music to what is happening. The words (content) often fit the formal structure closely, while the music (process) can be understood only in terms of the informal structure. Thus, assembly-line workers are almost certain to perform assembly-line tasks (content) as the organization chart suggests, but the interaction among them (process) may be different than expected. To truly understand what is going on in a work group, then, one must understand the elements of group process.

The foundations of group process are *goals, norms, structure,* and *identity*. A clear understanding of what happens in these four areas can lead to an accurate diagnosis of what's taking place in a group and why. Such a diagnosis has two uses: it enables one to predict future behavior (groups generate predictable interaction) and to anticipate the results of change. Without these insights one "flies blind."

Goals

One of the most used, abused, and misused pair of words in the jargon of group dynamics is "goal setting." Goal setting is a frequent and consistent problem in organizations: they lack clear, concise, relevant goals that can be communicated to and understood by individuals by means of measurable benchmarks of performance. This problem exists despite the fact that most individuals, groups, and organizations profess to have very clear goals.

The real dilemma involves the quality of goals. If a goal does not provide a means of measurement it is useless. If groups or individuals within an organization have different goals, much energy will be dissipated unproductively. The net result is "warm fuzzies" rather than crisp targets, split objectives rather than common goals, or both.

To illustrate this, take a vertical slice of an organization and ask a person at each level what his or her goal is. The result is likely to be something like this:

> *President:* "To make a profit."
> *Middle Manager:* "To meet my budget."
> *Worker:* "To earn a good living."

Note that there is a commonality among these responses. All are concerned with money in some way. But the *value*, at least the psychological value, of money is much different to these three people. The one common denominator is the matter of survival. This presents us with Rule 4.

> *Rule 4:* The primary objective of any group is to main-
> tain its orderly existence.

Survival is the only goal that "fits" across an entire organization, which largely explains why profit is a poor measure of success for those who have little impact on it.

Consider the case of Flexipack, a small manufacturer of plastic packaging materials. The Vice-President of Operations had just informed his managers that the "goal" for the coming year would be a 6 percent profit before taxes. There were no objections. A consultant then intervened to ask them the following questions:

1. When your department runs an order, do you know how much profit is generated?
2. Do you have complete control over the results?

The answer to both questions was an unequivocal "No!" Yet, they were willing to "buy into" performance toward a goal that they could neither measure nor control. Why did the managers remain silent? The answer to *that* question is written in the organization's history. Every year, goals are set, goals are missed, explanations offered, and explanations accepted. When the final numbers are computed to be "bad," the company hires itself a new Vice-President of Operations. Indeed, the current VP is the fourth in as many years. Of course, the managers all remain the same. After all, they are not to blame.

Were Flexipack an isolated case, one could write it off as a rare example of bad management. Unfortunately, goals are set only for the sake of setting goals—rather than to provide direction and control—in all too many organizations. The net result is businesses that don't know what business they are in.

In the case of Flexipack, the "business" of the operations function was to manufacture products against a set of standards, which included labor costs, overhead, and scrap rate. Profitability was irrelevant (an irreverent statement, but true). When run to standard, lack of profitability for a particular order would be a function of pricing (sales responsibility) but not of manufacturing.

To summarize, every group has goals, which aim to meet the needs of its members who are dependent upon it. When these needs are inconsistent with the group's stated formal goals, there will be dissonance. The group will act to meet its own needs, and the hell with the organization. Besides, it's kind of exciting to break in a new boss every year.

Norms

When groups group, they demonstrate predictable behavior, largely because control is exerted through the development of *norms*. Norms are rules that designate particular behaviors, attitudes, or beliefs to which people must adhere if they wish to continue their membership in a particular group. When it is understood by a work group that no one will produce more than a given standard, even though management requests more, a norm exists. It is measurable, clearly understood, and attainable. Thus, norms function in reality the way goals function in theory. When goals and norms are congruent, there is music. When they are not, there are words, many of which are of the four-letter variety.

To fully understand the concept of norms, one must also understand the notion of values. Values are ideas people hold as hopes and assumptions in the form of an ideal, a standard, a belief, or a goal so encompassing as to be unattainable. In the Flexipack example, profitability was a value, not a norm—something the company strove for but no one expected to attain.

Structure

Ask a manager about organizational structure and he or she is quick to pull out an organization chart that illustrates reporting relationships. The dilemma is that just as goals (values) do not reflect norms, neither does a formal reporting structure reflect how people interact. Once again we must dip into our semantic grab bag to distinguish between theory and reality, in this case between formal and informal structure.

A sample organization chart is shown in Figure 3. With the boxes empty it represents a crisp, neat representation of structure. Organization charts reflect content, not process. Put real people in these boxes and you begin to wrestle with the process issues of role, authority, and status. It is these issues that will quickly and clearly separate reality from intentions.

Role is a set of expectations that people have about the behavior of a person in a position. Since expectations will differ between people, so will their perceptions of a role. Thus, there will be a *prescribed role* (assumed via the organization chart), a *perceived role* (how the person in that position wants to be seen), and the *actual role* (how others truly see the person). The difference between these is often a function of *authority* and *status,* the former being the ability to get people to do something they don't want to do and the latter a value judgment about relative worth in a hierarchy.

A prime example of how these all come together but do not always fit is the job of foreman. Based on a formal organization chart, he or she has a clear leadership role with specific authority

Figure 3.   An organization chart.

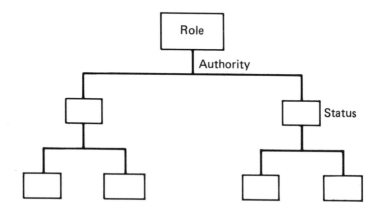

and some status relative to nonsupervisory positions. But reality shapes up a bit differently. Often the foreman is not permitted to hire, fire, reward, or discipline subordinates. With little authority, his or her role becomes that of taskmaster rather than people manager. In addition, the salaried first-line supervisor often earns less than he or she did as an hourly worker who could receive overtime pay. No wonder, then, that the job is accorded little or no status. Indeed, the offer of such a position as a reward for excellent individual performance must go down as management's biggest con game, in which both sides eventually lose.

Identity

One of the most interesting aspects of group formation is an almost immediate change in internal and external perception. Once people have accepted membership in a group, they begin to desensitize themselves to their group's flaws and accentuate the negative aspects of competing groups. This marked change illustrates the process of group identity and the "we-they" phenomenon that develops.

In the past, this process worked to the advantage of business organizations. People were tied to their jobs through company loyalty. Many of them defined their own identity through their work roles, suppressing most of their conflicting wants and needs. But attitudes are changing. Younger workers are not making the organizational commitments that underlie strong identity with a work group. Instead, they are meeting more of their needs through membership in groups outside of work—reflected in the increasing importance of leisure time and the greater emphasis on career planning and career changing that focuses on self rather than group.

Glass Targets

There is an old joke about a policeman who was found dragging a dead horse onto Main Street. When asked why he was performing this unpleasant task, he replied that it would make his report easier to write as he was a poor speller. Questioned further, he revealed that the horse had actually died on Kosciuszko Street.

Too often, organizations are equally guilty of distorting reality for the sake of simplicity. It is as if facts pass through glass that bends their image into fiction and fantasy (see Figure 4). The message should be clear by now. To understand what goes on in groups, one must have an undistorted view of the proceedings. A major way to do so is to focus on behavior rather than artifacts—that is, on the process variables rather than the content issues. We learn this lesson as children but forget it as adults—believe what you see, not what you are told—and it is the source of a child's charm and an effective manager's magic. They can see what is there, not what is supposed to be there—whether it be the emperor's new clothes or a profit motive for manufacturing. Look closely and you will see Rule 4 in action.

If you need proof, try this experiment. Observe a group that does not know you and over whom you have no authority. Focus on behavior (process) only. Write down your perception of goals, norms, informal structure, and identity.

Figure 4. **Glass targets.**

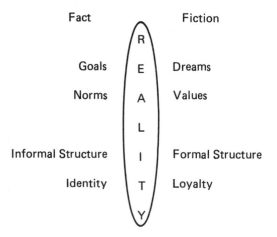

Fact		Fiction
	R	
Goals	E	Dreams
Norms	A	Values
	L	
Informal Structure	I	Formal Structure
Identity	T	Loyalty
	Y	

Then speak with the group's leader about his or her perception of organizational goals, philosophy (values), structure, and loyalty. The resulting differences may surprise you, as you have peeked behind the glass and looked closely at real group behavior.

If you are really daring, you might confront the leader with the dissonance between the two views. But don't expect a gush of appreciation for your insight. Instead, be prepared for a barrage of rationalizations attempting to point out how your perception was distorted. You are now firmly planted on the horns of the consultant's dilemma. Between them loom glass targets, twisting and bending each piece of dialogue, as you squint to see what you know is not there.

If all this sounds a bit unreal, consider the impact of a traditional attitude survey. Management, eager to know what is going on, sends out questionnaires to see through the glass. When the news is bad, the computerized report is quickly filed away for study and reflection; in essence it is buried. The moral: don't look at things you are unprepared to see.

There is an alternative. You can invite managers to look at the reality of their group's behavior and learn from it. It is a hard, painful process that requires strong commitment to excellent performance. For some it is worth the price.

3

Organizational
Behavior

*A camel is a horse designed by a
committee.*   Famous biologist

A great deal has been written about groups and organizations,
but little distinction has been made between the two. Indeed, for
some an organization is simply a group of groups. For others there is
a qualitative judgment, as in "let's get organized." When individuals
form groups to accomplish tasks, the groups are often vulnerable to
the loss of key members, particularly in new businesses and start-up
situations. In such a group, which is likely to be lean and tight with
respect to personnel, each person represents a huge resource. If the
group grows and prospers it begins to build an organization.

> *Rule 5:* An organization is a group that can survive the
> loss of any one member.

This rule is a very hard-nosed definition of what an organization
is and is not. It is meant to shatter a number of myths surrounding
groups that masquerade as organizations. For example, when a
large European manufacturer of typewriters purchased a similar
American firm for $8 million, it assumed it was also buying an
organization. Too late it discovered an empty shell from which talent had fled and where deadwood remained. The cost of replacing

the talent and rebuilding the organization eventually reached $80 million.

The history of mergers and acquisitions is filled with such horror stories. Even individuals regularly get "burned" when they wake up to the fact that they have paid an exorbitant price for a bit of capital equipment that was useless without the "genius" who made it work. What good are all those lovely checkered tablecloths when the chef is gone? Who cares about the chic décor when the top hairdresser is about to open her own shop?

The emergence of an organization out of a work group can be a thing of beauty either by design or by metamorphosis. Fast-food restaurants, in which transfer of management is often silky smooth, are an excellent example of the former. Family businesses that have successfully grown beyond the limits of the founding genius illustrate the latter. In each case the critical variable is vulnerability to the loss of individual talent. The process by which organization takes place involves three key elements: style, hierarchy, and control.

Process Style

A major contributor to the long-held belief that the world is flat was no doubt the ease with which it could be depicted on a two-dimensional surface such as parchment or paper. It may also be true that the simplicity of traditional pyramidal organization charts is a major reason why they have that shape. To begin at the beginning, most organizations are founded by at least two people. Even Henry Ford had a partner in the early days. It was his partner who was primarily responsible for setting up the first dealership organization.

In the usual case, one person makes the product or performs the service, while the other person sells it. Thus, there is an "inside" person and an "outside" person. If there were an organization chart it would look like a barbell, as depicted in Figure 5.

Figure 5. The birth of an organization.

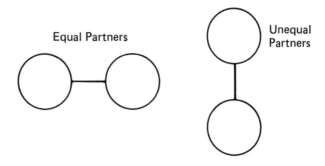

Even with increases in nonsupervisory personnel, the management structure remains the same—horizontal for equal partners and vertical when one individual maintains control. When managers are added, the issue of style begins to reach critical mass. Essentially there are three general process styles—autocracy, committee, and team—which are illustrated in Figure 6. Each represents a different constellation that reflects how the processes of leadership and power are dealt with.

In an autocratic style, the hub of the "wheel" may be an elected leader (by the group), a selected leader (by an outsider), or a self-elected leader who takes center stage as his or her due for some reason (such as having control of the stock). All processes go through this leader, and interaction tends to be one-on-one with the "boss." Should he or she leave for any reason, the group would most likely collapse. This style is typical of the "one-man band" that is acquired by a conglomerate, which then tries to play music with a new conductor. The result is often a great deal of noise. A variation on this theme is the "power behind the throne" syndrome.

In this case, the leadership function is not nearly as critical as the special expertise of one individual—say, a design engineer, a supersalesperson, or a gourmet chef. Without that person, the group cannot function effectively.

In both examples, the autocratic style fosters vulnerability either through the power of central leadership or irreplaceable ex-

Figure 6.   Process styles: (a) an autocracy; (b) a power behind the throne, a variation of an autocracy; (c) a committee; (d) a team.

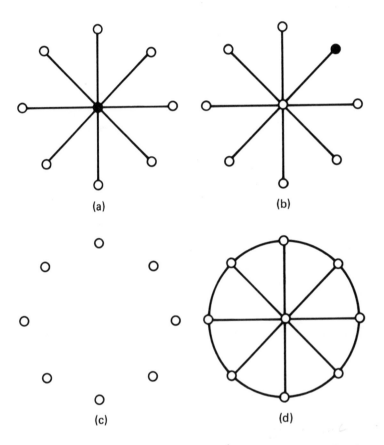

(a)   (b)

(c)   (d)

pertise. Thus, it is a group, not an organization (see Rule 5). It should be pointed out that there is a significant reward for individuals in these vital positions to maintain such a structure; their security is almost guaranteed. But it's not much fun for the other members of the group, who feel their lesser status sharply. Further, productivity is severely limited by the availability of the superstar's time and effort.

In some ways a committee is the antithesis of an autocracy.

Rather than power being too sharply focused, it is too softly diffused. In essence, a committee is a free-form group that often lacks leadership. There may be a chairperson, but he or she rarely has much power. The result is the formation of cliques and splinter groups that generate heat and light, but only a fraction of this energy is put to productive use. As in a molecule, if one atom is removed, the whole structure changes.

Team function is one of those marvelous concepts that looks great on paper but rarely gets off the ground. It is based on the notion of shared leadership and a balance of power. As Figure 6 illustrates, such a structure is capable of both the sharply focused direction of an autocracy and the free-form interaction of the committee. The basis of such functioning is that the group has a common goal and meets regularly to solve problems. More often, however, supposed teams have *similar* goals and meet regularly to *share* information. The risk of teamwork is that it is a time-consuming process. The payoff is that *all* of the group's resources can be brought to bear on any single problem. Also, it is far less vulnerable to the loss of any one member, including the formal leader.

Hierarchy

The preceding illustrations focused on how individuals interact in a group. Such issues are those of process, or *how* work gets done. A more common notation system, the organization chart, does an effective job of illustrating content issues—that is, *what* work gets done. Error creeps in when the content is assumed to describe the process.

Hierarchy is partly a result of the need to divide work among individuals in a group. Such division takes place because tasks are either too large or too complex for one person to do. A second reason for hierarchy is the perceived need for unity of command— for each person to have only one boss. The resulting structure is under constant stress from these two opposing forces. On the one hand there is a need for specialization of tasks, and yet there must

Figure 7.   The organizational force field.

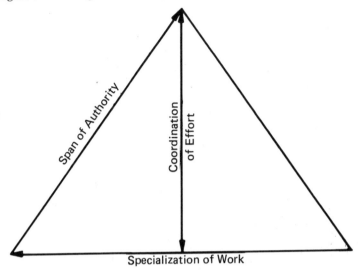

Span of Authority

Coordination of Effort

Specialization of Work

be coordination of effort. Factor in span of authority, or the maximum number of people a manager can physically supervise, and an organizational "force field" begins to emerge (see Figure 7).

The dilemma of organization charts is that they are marvelous schematics for task performance but poor blueprints for group behavior. To fully understand how an organization functions, one must keep two sets of books—one for content and one for process. To see this point illustrated, look at the hypothetical organization chart in Figure 8. Although it is unlikely that any one organization would be so structured, the chart does display the full range of task divisions. They are:

1. by function (President)
2. by territory (Sales)
3. by product (Production)
4. by process (Product A)
5. by customer (Product B)
6. by time (Product C)

When you put a person in each of these managerial boxes,

Figure 8. An organization chart.

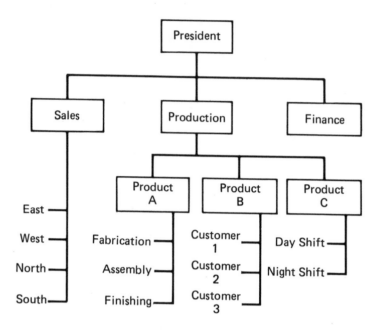

choices become evident. The objective for each manager is to pro-vide effective control while maintaining the appropriate division of labor within a realistic span of authority—to maximize the force field so that there is movement in a positive direction.

Control

The major rationale underlying the hierarchical structure of organi-zations is the imposibility of controlling large groups of people with diverse specialties in any other way. On a large scale, this is a mathematical fact of life. But within work groups, it is *not* the case.

The President: All options are open: autocracy, committee, and team. Each style may be successful, depending on the situation. Indeed all three may be used as illustrated in this table:

Task	Process	Result
Establish expected return on investment	Autocracy	A nonnegotiable directive
Identify markets	Committee	Creative "brainstorming"
Build operating plan	Team	Commitment to the plan

The "fact" that top management is functionally structured has little impact on how the group will behave.

The Sales Vice-President: Geographic division of labor is quite typical for a sales group. Indeed, it makes a great deal of sense in terms of the tasks involved. What does not make sense is an attempt to operate as a team or committee. Goals may be similar, but they are not held in common. Each territory is independent, succeeding or failing on its own merits. Bringing managers together to solve problems is an exercise in futility. Thus, national sales meetings inform, educate, and entertain. Problem solving remains in the lap of the individual manager.

The Production Vice-President: When there is little overlap in the manufacturing process, it may make sense to divide tasks by product. Here, too, an autocratic structure is reasonable, as product managers are not likely to have much commonality.

Product Manager A: The most typical specialization of labor in a production operation is based on manufacturing process or equipment. The key element is that it is *sequential*, raw product moving through each functional area until it reaches final form. Coordination of effort becomes essential, and teamwork can provide huge benefits in terms of productivity. On the other hand, autocratic control can squeeze the very life out of such an operation.

Product Manager B: On rare occasions, production operations will specialize by customer. Such a situation most often reflects a huge volume distributed across relatively few buyers. The amount of differentiation between products will determine the most efficient management structure. With great diversity of products this becomes a variation of product specialization.

Product Manager C: In an effort to get more use out of over-head costs, many production facilities operate more than one shift. Because there is duplication of function, product, territory, and customer, the opportunity for coordination through team structure is obvious. Alas, shifts are too often treated as if they exist in different worlds.

The Finance Vice-President: In an earlier section of this chapter it was pointed out that the birth of an organization was often a division of labor between production and sales (see Figure 5). Actually, there is a third function, that of finance. All organizations engage in these three basic activities no matter what their specific business. They must produce goods or services, market them, and finance the production and sales operations. The omission of the finance function points out the special dilemma of a staff function. In a newborn enterprise, financial activity tends to be relegated either to spare time (nights and weekends) or spare people (relatives and friends).

When a full-time professional is placed in this position, he or she will bear the brunt of the process style adopted by the top management group. It is the usual lot of a staff manager to be caught between the need to specialize and the lack of power to coordinate. The result in this case will determine whether he or she functions as a financial ally or a dispirited "bean counter."

Organizational Climate

Like the weather, the shape and texture of what goes on in organizations are much measured but poorly predicted. Yet, to discard what is known in favor of "gut feeling" is as foolish as relying on one's bunions to determine the likelihood of rain. Indeed, to dwell on what we do not know is often to ignore how much we do.

Management and meteorology are games of chance. They rely on probability rather than precision. People often have a great deal of difficulty with that which is not completely predictable. They quickly forget a marvelous batting average in one awful streak of strike-outs.

The climate of an organization is the result of a delicate and complex balance between individuals, groups, and their interactions. Organizations are living, breathing things that are in a constant state of flux.

To measure such a thing is to examine not only mass but energy and direction. As a minimum, consider these five factors:

1. *History*. The background and experience of an organization, like that of individuals, will severely restrict the array of decisions that it will make in the future. Successful "go-go" performers are unlikely to keep taking huge risks in the marketplace. It is more often the stodgy old-timers who are going to try something new; or better yet, they let some young upstart test the water and, if he or she is successful, they then move in with their big bucks. There are exceptions, of course, but they are rare.

2. *Culture*. From tribal village to executive suite there are patterns and personalities that cling to a group of people who live and work together. Watch the young "comers" and they will tell you true. Do they emulate the slick, three-piece-suited marketeers? Or is it the slightly rumpled engineer-scientist who is honored by the council of the elders? Listen carefully to their dreams and values, but keep your eyes sharply focused on their goals and norms.

3. *Technology*. Traditionally this area of organizational diagnosis has been ignored by behavioral scientists. Yet, it is a major determinant of organizational climate. No amount of management magic will maintain a product or service that doesn't perform or that has outlived its usefulness. More important, examine such fascinating phenomena as margin, market share, and leverage. There is a family-owned pickle company in the Northeast that is superbly managed but lives from hand to mouth in the shadow of the big food processors. At the same time, there is a poorly managed manufacturer of one small piece of laboratory equipment. It so controls the market that orders gush in from all over the world, and it reaps handsome profits as well.

4. *Structure*. A significant chapter in organizational history was written many years ago when Sears Roebuck went to a flat (decentralized) structure and began to whip all of its nearest competitors. Store managers were given great autonomy in running their own businesses. They were encouraged to function as entrepreneurs rather than as automatons. But the hand of fate, having written, moved on. Recently, a top executive of a highly successful retail chain said that he is able to walk into any of his stores blindfolded and place his hand on the same product in the same place. The age of cloning is upon us with all of its pitfalls and payoffs. It is a unique solution to the organizational dilemma of vulnerability. Also it is another example of keeping what works (flat structure) and discarding what doesn't (independence of product mix).

The keys to process structure have been identified as role, authority, and status. The result may be an autocracy, a committee, or a team. Even in the cookie-cutter world of retail merchandising, some store managers retain a unique bit of authority. They can lower prices to any level they choose from "loss-leader" to downright giveaway. Thus, all of the lessons learned by Sears have not been discarded.

In organizational life, as in life in general, we deal with successive approximations, cutting and fitting to see what works. Education is slow and painful; usually we learn more about what doesn't work than what does. Problems of structure most often result from muscle and sinew that have outgrown their skeleton. Rare is the organization that has a structure waiting in the wings for tomorrow's challenges. Organizational structure is more likely to be a brittle framework designed around a unique set of people who cannot or will not change. Built for content, it outgrows the emerging process.

5. *Group Dynamics*. The dynamics of group behavior involve a crazy bit of arithmetic in which two plus two may equal five or, on a bad day, three. A team of old pros who work well together will almost always beat a group of all-stars pulling in their own different directions. Thus, the sum total of talent in an organization tells us less than we would like to know about final output. Group behavior

is not additive but is the result of a delicate balance that protects the group's orderly existence (Rule 4). Conflict is the energizer of group behavior in which even small changes may cause great movement. When the conflict is one of ideas, creativity will result such that there is a positive energy flow. When the conflict is among people, productivity will suffer greatly as forces cancel each other out.

This does not mean that team structure is always the answer. When tasks are highly routine and repetitive, an authoritarian approach will often be more effective. In such a case there is no expectation of synergy, in which the whole is equal to more than its parts. Rather, the goal is to reduce error through tight control. An assembly line is not the place to be creative, a fact that has been the tragedy of the supplanting of craftsmanship by cheap labor and of the great success of packaged franchises.

Even a committee structure has its place in the sun. When the process is exceedingly more important than the content, such a structure may afford a large number of people the opportunity to speak and be heard. Thus, where roles are unclear and authority is vague, the committee bestows status on a bunch of folks who want and need it—a dandy design for a "rap session" but a poor choice for accomplishing a task. Notice that while most volunteer organizations have huge memberships, only a handful does the actual work. Appropriately named, these *task forces* get the work done; the rest of the operation is ceremonial.

Thus, group dynamics is an interaction between the *conflict* of differing individual levels of motivation and the *need to control* behavior to accomplish tasks. This, in a nutshell, is the dilemma that faces every manager, from shop foreman to corporation president.

Reflections

Organizations are a reflection of the people who create and maintain them. They are a microcosm of a society, complete with a history, culture, and technology all their own. To understand how people and groups function within them, you have to understand these three factors and the resulting structure. They form the arena within which the management game is played. The only consistent attribute one can assign them is Rule 6.

Rule 6: Organizations exist to survive.

Given this rule, it is vital that one be very clear about the playing conditions. Students of the game talk about "open systems," which is jargon for the fact that organizations do not exist in a vacuum but are constantly interacting with the rest of the world. In Part II we will look at this interaction. The name of the game is process, internal and external. We will examine it in some detail.

PART II

PROCESS

It's not whether you win or lose but how you play the game.

Famous bookie

4

The Role of
the Manager

*Good pitching will defeat good hitting
and vice versa.*   Famous manager

I am frankly amazed. Writers have been dissecting the role of managers since the dawn of the Industrial Revolution. From Fayol and Gulick to Likert and Argyris, lists have been drawn and redrawn. Yet the guy on the line is as confused as ever about what he is supposed to do. Perhaps it is time to admit that dissection is not the answer. After all, you can take your car apart and put it back together without increasing your driving skill one iota. And therein lies the rub—we have once again focused on the simple (the car) rather than the complex (the driver). The result is a great deal of knowledge about what *should* be done but very little about what *is* done. Most of us know where our hands should be on the steering wheel, but few of us put them there. Chris Argyris comes the closest to the truth when he talks about *espoused theory* versus *theory in use*—that is, the difference between what we say and what we do.

Why is there a difference? Because whether you are managing a bank or driving a truck, you are dealing with probabilities. Most theories seem to focus on how to build an organization rather than how to run one that is already there. The roles of manager and truck driver involve not construction but delivery—to get the goods out whether they be hamburgers or hangar doors. Rules, regulations, and potholes make the job interesting, but they don't tell you how to get it done. That's where management and truck driving come in.

Probability, Preparation, and People

I have seen people who can't add play blackjack. I have watched rational men draw to an inside straight. I have consulted with manufacturing operations that had no performance standards. Numbers frighten some people and that's a shame, but for those who manage, lack of measurement can be disastrous. Management, like all games of chance, is the process of making the best out of what you've got. If you can't keep score, you are dead before you start. If you can, it's a beginning, but a very small one. To paraphrase an old maxim, an ounce of prevention is worth a ton of putting out fires.

Gambling and managing are surrounded by an incredible number of myths. There is the gambler's fallacy, which argues that if a tossed coin has come up heads 100 times in a row, the bettor should take tails (wrong). And there is the manager's fallacy that technical expertise is a substitute for people-oriented skills (wrong).

Probability is the base line of poker. It is a starting point, not an end. Preparation involves knowing beforehand exactly what action will be taken for a whole host of situations and working contingency plans for specific players who tend to behave in certain ways.

Likewise, productivity is the base line of management. It, too, is but a start. Preparation involves considerable thought and study before a single card is turned. The illogic of people, groups, and organizations precludes a purely actuarial approach to improving performance.

Figure 9.   **The productivity dilemma.**

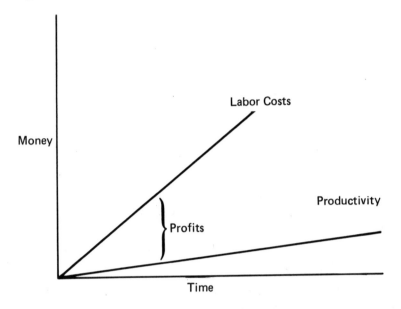

Productivity

The dilemma that faces all managers is illustrated in Figure 9. Productivity (defined as output per person) continues to increase only marginally while labor costs have skyrocketed. The result is a squeeze on profits and a challenge to the skill and ingenuity of managers. To increase profit they have but three choices: raise productivity, reduce labor costs, or increase prices. Current rates of inflation show that the last road is the one that is too often taken.

To repeat, a manager is one who delivers the goods in spite of people, potholes, and problems. To do so at a profit one must control productivity and costs, whether they are measured in dollars, doughnuts, or dented fenders. And to do this, one must be prepared. The skill involved is planning, which is the very core of a manager's role.

Planning

A recent newspaper article described a man who crossed a bridge each day on his way to work. As he looked down on the river rushing below, he wondered what he would do if he saw a person drowning and chose to jump to the rescue. Since he had no answer, he contacted a diving school and presented the problem to them. He now has an answer (hit the water straight up, feet first, then tuck). Planning is crossing a bridge you may never get to. It is anticipating the consequences of one's actions rather than reacting to circumstances as they occur.

The problem with planning is not in its complexity but in its rarity. It just isn't done very often. It is a learned skill that does not get taught. We say we will "cross that bridge when we get to it" and then cross it poorly, if at all.

To get down to basics, the process of planning involves a simple three-step strategy:

1. What is the current situation?
2. What should it be?
3. What, if anything, must be done to change it?

The key word here is *change*. Those who plan know that nothing remains the same. Those who don't, wish it were not so. Such is the difference between a potentially effective manager and one who hasn't got a chance.

This discussion may seem simplistic, but it isn't. Because of the nature of probabilities, there will always be times when luck wins out, when a solid game plan is insufficient to ovecome a stroke of fate. It is only *over time* that planning skill pays off. For the short haul, all we have is random results. The biggest fallacy of all is that success in one game is predictive of success in another.

The bottom line is that the central role of a manager is to plan. The fact that many don't does not discredit the concept but points out the difference between those who have the title and those who do the work.

Organizing

Organizing is the link between the planning and the doing aspects of the management process. Its symbols are depicted in the traditional organization chart. As was pointed out in Chapter 3, when the chart misrepresents reality by presuming to define process, it is less than useless. However, when the formal and informal structures are consistent such that both content and process are represented, it can be a useful tool. For most managers, organizing is more a matter of changing and reorganizing an existing structure than of developing a new one.

The traditional philosophy of organization as represented by formal organization charts is based on four assumptions about what is right and proper for process in a work group. They are:

1. *Division of work:* greater efficiency is achieved when people specialize in specific tasks.
2. *Unity of command:* coordination is easier when each person has one boss.
3. *Authority:* managers have the right to make decisions, assign tasks, and require satisfactory performance.
4. *Discipline:* subordinates will obey those in authority.

Simply stated, organizing is deciding who will do what in the achievement of an organization's objectives. Thus, it is tightly tied to the effectiveness of the planning function. Without clear, measurable goals, the effectiveness of a particular structure cannot be determined. When the above assumptions are not met, the value of the structure is greatly diminished even when goals are specific.

Problems in organizing tend to be the result of too great a focus on either tasks or people so that one excludes the other. Each extreme limits flexibility and, thus, the manager's ability to fit people to jobs. In addition, organizing often takes the blame when the true culprit is poor planning. Indeed, a good plan will often work even with poor organization, but the opposite is rarely true. A cumbersome organization may get the job done, but its productivity will be less than ideal.

Directing

Planning and organizing are both part of preparation. Through the directing function, though, the action needed to actually reach objectives is launched and maintained. It is this function that most clearly rests on the manager's ability to deal with people-oriented issues both individually and in groups. The processes involved are those of communication, leadership, and motivation. The key dimension is *insight*—the ability to understand the behavior of oneself and others. A manager who is sensitive to "what is going on" can communicate clearly what he or she wants and have some assurance of being heard. Further, such a manager will be able to adopt a leadership style that has the greatest chance of influencing subordinates in the appropriate direction. Finally, one may just be able to establish an environment in which people's wants and needs are congruent with the goals and objectives of the organization. This is the *only* thing that can be done about motivation in the workplace.

Controlling

Of all the aspects of a manager's role, controlling tends to be the least understood because, in a sense, it is based on a negative hypothesis—that is, the finest planning, organizing, and directing will miss the target unless there are midcourse corrections. This is heightened by the fact that managers are rarely evaluated on their ability but rather on their results. As one top executive said, "Don't give me managers who are great problem solvers, give me managers who don't have any problems." And therein lies the dilemma of the manager's role. Success depends on the ability to plan, organize, direct, *and* control. But, results are invariably the only measures of talent that carry any weight. Unjust perhaps, but a reality never-theless.

The objective of control is to change behavior. In a more general sense, controls are designed to create order out of the diverse interests and potentially diffuse behaviors of group members.

At a cognitive level it is a rather straightforward concept. But, alas, we are dealing with people, and the notion of control is highly charged with emotion, and for good reason. In spite of all the data to the contrary, organizations continue to try to change behavior through the threat of punishment. Pick up any set of rules and regulations that relate to an organization and you will surely find yourself staring at a list of "don'ts" and "shouldn'ts." Only recently, under the catch phrase "behavior modification," have some managers grudgingly accepted the value of positive reinforcement.

Control is the function that is most affected by process structure, where the payoff for the right structure for the right situation comes into play. A key variable is that of *influence*. A team structure affords members maximum influence, and when combined with strong control, it can yield very high productivity. On the other hand, an authoritarian structure also has strong control, but its influence among members is minimal. The result is often significantly lower productivity. Finally, a committee structure entails considerable influence among members but control is often lacking. The effects of structure, control, and influence on productivity are summarized in the following table:

Structure	Control	Member Influence	Productivity: Tasks Complex	Productivity: Tasks Routine
Team	Strong	Strong	High	Low
Authoritarian	Strong	Weak	Low	High
Committee	Weak	Strong	Low	Low

Notice that the impact on productivity is highly dependent on the complexity of the task. A team structure on the assembly line may increase the workers' satisfaction (because they have greater influence), but it is unlikely to increase productivity. Indeed, the additional time investment may never be returned in terms of output.

Conclusions

The dilemma of defining a manager's role stretches between the ideal of measuring skills and the reality of accepting results. The "fact" that a work group performs superbly—or poorly—may or may not reflect the ability of its manager. Part of the problem is that "performance" tends to be a relative concept in organizations. Unlike baseball, there is no way to know when a manager is having a winning season. All we have are comparative judgments against a subjective goal. When that goal is meaningful and realistic, then and only then will the definition and assessment of a manager's role have real value.

An example of this dilemma occurs often in sales organizations. Branch A gets an unsolicited inquiry that results in a significant piece of business. So important is this business that the branch receives all of the company's accolades and the branch manager is dubbed a star. Branch B, on the other hand, through a slow and steady rebuilding process, misses its quota by only a small margin but shows good potential. It receives no awards, and the manager is told to redouble the effort. In this way, the results of an organization's activity mask the true ability of a manager. Consider Rule 7.

Rule 7: A manager's role is to achieve desired results.

First and foremost, one must understand how score will be kept and who will keep it. Managers must be able to look at those glass targets with the sun at their backs. Then they can plan, organize, direct, and control for maximum results. Or a manager can step up to the plate unprepared and flail away. He or she might even get lucky and hit a home run. After all, it's only a game.

References

Argyris, Chris, *Increasing Leadership Effectiveness*. New York: John Wiley, 1976.

Fayol, Henri (translated by Constance Storrs), *General and Industrial Management*. London: Pitman, 1949.

Gulick, Luther, ed. (with L. F. Urwick), *Papers on the Science of Administration*. New York: Institute of Public Administration, 1937.

Likert, Rensis, *The Human Organization*. New York: McGraw-Hill, 1967.

5

Work Groups

I gave at the office. Famous blood donor

In Chapter 2, groups in general were discussed and identified as having three distinguishing features: goals, norms, and structure. In this chapter we will begin to zero in on special functional groups in organizations. Bear in mind that these functions are generic and may not be labeled as such. That is, a "sales" clerk is rarely called upon to sell, while a banker may spend a great deal of time attracting new customers.

In the executive suite these differences are much more subtle but equally true. I recall the president and executive vice-president of a billion-dollar conglomerate who had developed a marvelously compatible working relationship. The president was a brilliant tax accountant and spent considerable energy dealing with the investment community. Meanwhile, the vice-president, who was a "shirt-sleeves" engineer, flew from plant to plant to keep up with what was going on "in the trenches." It was as if they had consciously divided up the role of top manager: you take planning and organizing, I'll handle direction and control. It was like a good marriage in which coordination becomes almost instinctive.

Function

There is a heavy message in the traditional adult-to-child query, "What do you want to *be* when you grow up?" It reflects our society's preoccupation with title and status rather than process and substance. We tend to focus on *being* rather than *doing*. Thus, it becomes difficult at times to figure out just what people are doing. In this section we will look at the "doing" aspect of work groups. Here, then, are the major functional specialties that arise in organizations.

Sales

The most striking aspect of the behavior of people who sell is that they can't seem to turn it off. Blessed with a strong ego and a need to convince others, they are often masters at playing games—the reason being that they pay very close attention to the rules. While you and I seek to perfect our putting stroke, they are pondering how to raise their handicap and thus increase their leverage should a friendly bet arise.

Every organization, regardless of product or service, for profit or not, involves the sales function. Those that forget this function will, in the long run, cease to exist. The lack of selling behavior in sales clerks in quite understandable when you consider their role. They are paid minimum wage with no incentive to make a sale. Retail organizations that recognize this fact (such as discount stores) have done away with the position—a prime example of a manager hitting the right target by applying Rule 7 (a manager's role is to achieve desired results).

In contrast, consider this dialogue that actually took place recently:

Customer:	I'd like to see a typewriter.
Sales Clerk:	We have three.
Customer:	Which do you recommend?
Sales Clerk:	I don't know.
Customer:	What features does the most expensive one have?
Sales Clerk:	An instruction book comes with it.
Customer:	*(after trying out typewriter)* Does this come in pica?
Sales Clerk:	Huh?

> *Customer:*   *(getting angry)* Do you know anything about type-
> writers?
> *Sales Clerk:*   I'd better get the manager.

The dysfunction between goals and norms in sales is both funny and sad, and it appears at all levels. Corporate Goliaths have been toppled by aggressive Davids when they ignored the threat of competition. Stuck with a group of "order takers," they discovered too late that they no longer had an exclusive market. Such is the warning of Rule 8.

> *Rule 8:* When goals and norms disagree, change the
> structure.

Both the photocopier and computer industries learned this lesson the hard way. With the advent of desk-top copiers and minicomputers, significant structural changes were forced upon the giants of these businesses.

Marketing

Although marketing is often used as a synonym for sales, as a generic function it is quite different. It is to planning and organizing what sales is to directing and controlling. The essence of marketing is knowing what business you are in or planning to be in. Business history is replete with items that did not sell because there was no market and those that ceased to sell because the market evaporated. Consider Edsels and railroad passenger service.

In spite of all the complex technology associated with marketing, it tends to be primarily a function of creativity, adaptability, and insight. No product or service sells itself, not even gold. On the other hand, there is a market for anything if it can be found. Thus, those old Edsels have been appreciating in value as collector's items.

The goals of marketing are to meet the needs of a customer and to create needs that were not previously apparent. The terms "business" and "customer" are not meant to imply that these are limited to for-profit organizations only. Notice that the March of Dimes keeps right on marching even though polio was cured over a decade ago—another instance of Rule 4 (the primary objective of a group is to maintain its orderly existence).

In spite of a great deal of study, very little is known about creative behavior. We do know, however, what it is not. People who approach tasks in rigid ways and require a great deal of structure are unlikely to produce innovative results—a strong argument for marketing departments to adopt a team process. Indeed, organizations that hang with a market that is going sour are almost always autocracies. As for committees, want to buy a camel?

Production

All organizations go through cycles of growth and decay. When the capacity to produce goods or services greatly exceeds sales volume, there is a tendency to ignore the production function. On the other hand, when orders are backlogged into infinity, great attention is paid to squeezing out one more widget. The net result is that production organizations constantly find themselves on the horns of a dilemma: when the opportunity for improving productivity exists (undersold conditions), no one is interested; when interest in productivity is at its peak (oversold conditions), the time is not available to try to increase it.

Nowhere is there greater disparity between goals and norms than in the production function. The graph in Figure 9 pointed clearly to the lack of productivity growth that results from this inequity. The real culprit is the traditional brittle structure that remains static while conditions cry out for change (Rule 8).

For nearly half a century behavioral scientists have tried to prove that employee satisfaction and job performance are directly connected. IT HAS NEVER BEEN DONE. The economic demands of a production operation are to produce more at less cost. These demands violate every rule of human behavior.

Rule 1: People always act in their own best interest,
given the facts as they know them, BUT people
are rarely given feedback on their performance. /

Rule 2: People act to meet perceived needs, BUT jobs
are dull, routine, and monotonous.

Rule 3: People meet needs by getting rewards and
avoiding punishment, BUT poor performance is
punished while good performance is ignored.

Rule 4: The primary objective of any group is to maintain its orderly existence, BUT productivity improvement threatens a group's sense of order.

To understand why this discrepancy exists is to understand the
structure of most production operations. Compare a first-line production supervisor with a first-line position in sales:

Role

Foreman: punished for a structure that does not work and does
not change.

Sales Manager: rewarded for the performance of others in a structure that remains fluid.

Authority

Foreman: constantly overruled by management, unions, and
government agencies.

Sales Manager: stands squarely between subordinates and supervisors with great freedom to act.

Status

Foreman: dress, pay, education, and upward mobility afford
little prestige.

Sales Manager: well-dressed, well-paid, and often educated so that
the job is a stepping stone to the executive suite.

With great fanfare, Volvo switched some production lines to
"work teams" that had responsibility for the construction of complete automobiles. Job satisfaction increased significantly as did the
quality of the product. Unfortunately profit margins slipped, and
the grand experiment was abandoned. General Motors went to the
other extreme and built a highly automated plant in Lordstown,

Ohio, that produced complete automobiles in one location. The result was a car that caused endless headaches for its owners and the eventual disappearance of that model (the Vega).

This is not to condemn these automakers for failing but rather to applaud them for trying. Any organization that doesn't modify its structure to meet changing needs will ultimately make awful music.

Research

Who can resist the romance and adventure of Tom Edison? As our most prolific inventor, Edison stands alone as a genius for developing products that could be efficiently manufactured, filled genuine needs (created markets), and sold like hot cakes. Such are the dreams that research and development departments are made of.

The reality of such endeavors is that even in Edison's day, organizations put great pressure on him to stop his foolishness and conform (Rule 4). That he did not is testimony to his compulsive need to tinker and create (Rule 2).

The goal of research is to develop new products or services. The norm is to develop new markets. Freddie Laker's no-frills airline service to Great Britain was as much the product of research as the steamboat or the jet engine.

The major issue for organizations is how to structure a function that by its very nature resists being structured. Indeed, creativity and organizations go together like oil and water. And Rule 5 supports this point. What group can survive the loss of a creative genius? The uniqueness of Edison was that he was both a creative scientist and a sound businessman. The probability of that occurring in one human being is minuscule.

Effective organizations have found three strategies to deal with this dilemma. Some seek out and purchase innovations while their inventors are still struggling. Thus, Hunt-Wesson owns Orville Redenbacher's Gourmet Popcorn (which quickly captured a majority share of the market). Others insulate their creative geniuses from the day-to-day frustrations of organizational life (the "think-tank"). A third strategy is to build a bridge between research and marketing: rather than buying or isolating creativity, it is built into the process. Not the structure, mind you, but the *process*. Research, like any other function, can be planned, organized, directed, and controlled. The key is to have someone manage it.

Consider this actual case. Phil was the Vice-President of Technical Services. He was greatly concerned about the performance of Hans, his recently promoted Director of Research. "Hans is not keeping up with the administrative end of the job," he admitted. "On top of that, he seems constantly tired and drawn." Further discussion revealed that Hans was returning at night to work in the lab. The answer seemed obvious: return Hans to the lab. Phil shook his head. "His pride would never allow him to do that. My only recourse is to fire him."

I met Hans in the lab that night. He was indeed tired but seemed relatively happy. "I hate my new job," he moaned, "it's just paperwork, paperwork, and more paperwork." "Why don't you ask to be put back in the lab?" I queried. "They would never let me do that," he answered.

In this case there was a happy ending. Hans is back in the lab doing his thing. A new manager—one whose expertise is in administration, not research—was placed in the director's job. The paperwork is flowing nicely. So is Hans.

Quality Control

The function of QC as it is traditionally performed in organizations is an exercise in frustration and futility. It is a game that cannot be won. Consider a cadre of inspectors whose job is to prevent "bad stuff" from going out the door. On paper, this is not such a bad idea. In reality, the folks who produce the "stuff" are given a visible enemy. Achieving quality standards becomes a quest to get it by the inspectors. If quality is acceptable, the organization begins to wonder if the function is overstaffed.

An aging superstar is often awarded a variety of staff jobs from radio announcer to coach. Never would management consider him for the job of umpire or referee. They know a losing proposition when they see one.

Walking through a plant recently, I was struck by the fact that, amongst all the grays and browns of machinery and boxes, there were bright red labels here and there proclaiming "REJECT." Like parking tickets flapping in the wind, they bear mute testimony to those who were caught. The function of quality control is a prime example of Rule 3 in action. Since people act to avoid punishment, they will act to avoid the punishers as well. Far from being part of the team, the inspection department is often an organizational leper colony.

Some businesses, like medical products, are required by law not only to have a QC function but to insist that the department not report to the production operation. Since we are a democracy, the inspectors are not required to wear armbands.

A recent "innovation" has been to change the name of this function to *quality assurance*. The intent was to make the role of inspector less punitive. Hardly anyone was fooled.

Maintenance

The dilemma of the maintenance function is a variation of the previous one. While QC is often set up as a passive enemy, the maintenance function tends to be an active one. When a machine breaks down or a pipe bursts, the expectation is that it will be fixed immediately. When it is not, the function becomes the recipient of much anger and a great deal of blame. On the other hand, when all is well, there is some discussion of how much time the mechanics spend drinking coffee. Notice that while the function draws considerable heat, no one suggests disbanding it in favor of an outside contractor. Such is the paradox of a necessary evil.

There is a marvelous commercial on television in which an auto mechanic fondles an oil filter as an alternative to an expensive valve job. His punch line is, "You can pay me now or pay me later." Such is the logic of preventive maintenance. Judging by actual behavior, it is a myth. Since the value of preventive maintenance has never been proved, the secret to family-car ownership is to sell the old bus before the valves begin to dance. And in factory gamesmanship, the plant manager holds the machinery together with spit and chewing gum while reaping the benefits of a fine return on assets of fully depreciated equipment—a splendid example of knowing how score is kept.

Finance

I once asked my father, who is a C.P.A., what an accountant did. He explained the job very simply as finding the mistakes of other people. And so another kibitzer is added to the game.

As an internal function, finance tends to be one of keeping score. Unlike the previous two staff functions, however, this one is often given considerable status. A wise game player knows enough to take good care of the guy who records his results. A foolish one may find himself the victim of an inventory re-evaluation. That's where you get caught carrying Nehru jackets and buggy whips at retail value rather than as junk.

As a member of a management team, the financial person can be a valuable ally. Unfortunately, many find or put themselves in an adversary position. As Keepers of the Exchequer, they sit with the key to the treasury dangling around their neck. They dare you to try and spend money.

The other extreme is illustrated by a cartoon in a financial magazine.

Personnel Manager:	I'd like you to meet Joe, he's a candidate for our controller job.
President:	Joe, how much is two plus two?
Joe:	What would you like it to be?
President:	You're hired!

There may be some truth to accusations of creative accounting, but as any good game player knows, the rules haven't really been defined until you see how far they will bend. An ounce of loophole is often worth a ton of production.

Engineering

A fairly accurate definition of the engineering function might be the science of the possible. As of this writing, a major auto maker is facing bankruptcy. Much attention is being paid to functions such as sales, marketing, and finance. Lost in all this hoopla is the decision made years ago to lay off 5,000 engineers. Thus, while the spotlight is on rebates and loans, the owners and mechanics of these vehicles are tearing their hair out trying to deal with a whole host of design flaws.

On another front, some of the auto workers are picketing foreign-car dealerships claiming unfair competition. These foreign cars continue to sell well despite inflation, recession, and a weakening dollar. Who is buying these cars? A brief poll of friends, acquaintances, and clients indicates that for the most part it's the engineers. Consumer magazines that track frequency-of-repair records tend to back up their choices as well.

The point of this discussion is that the engineering function can often be a major factor in the survival of an organization. Indeed, in the past, one solution to the dilemma of poor productivity has been technological innovation. Rather than increase the effectiveness of people, machines were designed to replace them. There is increasing evidence that technology won't bail us out this time.

A case in point is Mediseal, a major producer of hospital equipment and supplies. One of its product lines was assembled at a large piece of equipment called a carrousel. Eight middle-aged women positioned themselves around it and fitted parts together as it rotated. Although the process was a vast improvement over earlier ones, engineering came up with an even better machine. This one ran in a straight line from one operation to the next. Unfortunately productivity went down rather than up. Someone forgot Rule 2 (people act to meet perceived needs.)

At the carrousel the women were free to chat with each other as their fingers flew over the parts. For many, the meeting of social needs far outweighed those met by pay. The new machine isolated them from one another. As frustration set in, so did poor performance.

Personnel

What is the role of the personnel function in an organization? Peter Drucker suggests it is "partly a file clerk's job, partly a housekeeping job, partly a social worker's job, and partly 'firefighting,' heading off union trouble or settling it." Add to this the administrative burden of dealing with government legislation on a wide range of issues from equal employment opportunity to occupational safety and the water becomes muddier still. The bottom line is that there is no clear-cut definition. Indeed, one could make a sound argument that there can't be. The reality is that the personnel function most often becomes what the person responsible for it makes of it. The key variable seems to be the particular area of expertise people bring to the job. That is, whether the personnel director was formerly a file clerk or a firefighter will most likely determine the issues that he or she will address. Here are a few examples.

Joyce is the recently appointed personnel director of a large hotel. Her training and prior experience were in social work. She has quickly built marvelous rapport with the hourly work force. During a recent visit, she excused herself to help one of the dishwashers with a personal problem.

Danny is a personnel manager in a huge corporate headquarters. He has moved up fast and seems to always be at the right place at the right time. A majority of his time is spent meeting with executives in the company. Subordinates say he is bright and a master at politics. They also say one should never turn one's back on him.

Fred is the industrial relations manager of a small machine shop. In the past he has been general manager of a plant and run his own recruiting firm. Much of his time is spent finding young, trainable employees. The remainder is spent counseling them. He does not get along well with line management because he disagrees with how they run the plant.

In recent years the personnel function has come up with a new name, human resources, which has a nice ring but has done little to add clarity. Any organization that has or is considering such a function should give considerable time and attention to defining its role, particularly as it relates to power in the organization.

Power

A major process variable that runs through all of these functions is power. To work in an organization is to deal with it on an intimate, day-to-day basis. Sales functions almost always have power; personnel functions rarely do. Organizational power, like electricity, is both an illusion and a reality. Since one cannot deal with it directly, what is left is effect. The illusion is that there is something called an electron; the reality is what happens when you stick your finger in a light socket. Such is the nature of power in organizations. It is an illusion that has very real impact. To generate power, then, is to create an illusion. This is Rule 9.

> *Rule 9:* To gain power, act as if you have it; to lose it,
> act as if you don't.

In Chapter 2, organizational structure was shown to be a function of three process issues: role, authority, and status. These three issues will determine a function's power. Some organizations are known to be marketing-oriented, some engineering-oriented, others sales-oriented, and still others finance-oriented. These terms are euphemisms for where the power is perceived to be.

Note that rarely, if ever, is an organization seen to be powered by quality control, maintenance, personnel, or even research. At best, these functions are given more or less emphasis; but emphasis is not power. With unclear roles, limited authority, and low status they live in the twilight zone of organizational structure. In contrast, sales, marketing, production, and engineering tend to have somewhat defined roles, considerable authority, and relatively high status.

In organizational jargon, what we have defined is the difference between *line* and *staff* functions. But we have defined them in terms of process rather than of content. By doing so, it should become clear that the key to increasing the effectiveness of staff functions is power. More specifically, by clarifying roles, sharpening authority, and increasing status, these functions can be brought out into the sunshine. As an example, consider the following situation.

International Widgets was having a serious quality problem. Interviews with various departments revealed a variety of perceptions of what the problem was:

Sales:	It's production's fault; they just run for quantity.
Marketing:	Our competitors make a better product; it's a design problem.
Production:	It's sales's fault; they sell what we can't make.
Finance:	It's a pricing problem; we should charge more for the stuff.
Engineering:	It's the machines; they are old and worn out; we can't hold tolerances.
Maintenance:	It's production's fault; they won't let us maintain the equipment properly.
Research:	I don't understand; it worked in the lab.
Personnel:	It's the people; they just aren't motivated.
Quality Control:	Every time we reject an order, it's shipped anyway.

Notice that responsibility is passed around like a hot potato with one paradoxical exception—quality control. Such is the full meaning of adding insult to injury. In spite of the function being called "quality control," the problem of uncontrolled quality remains.

The solution in this case was to invoke Rule 8. Goals and norms were so far apart as to be in different worlds; the structure had to change. Two alternative strategies were developed. Plan A involved dissolving the quality control department and assigning inspectors to the production operation. The goal was to make production fully responsible for quality.

Plan B was to replace the quality control manager with a "hard hitter" who would be given considerable clout. His mission would be twofold—first, to reduce returns due to poor quality; second, and more important, to identify and correct the causes of poor quality. In actual fact, both courses were taken. The quality control department was disbanded, and a powerful new position was created with authority and status equivalent to the line organizations. Although quality problems haven't disappeared, they have been significantly reduced.

Scoring

There is an old saying that goes something like this: "Them that can, do; them that can't, teach; them that can't teach, administrate." The author was obviously a *doer* and had much to say about the role and status of those who aren't. The irony is that many who *do* can neither teach nor administrate. That was certainly the case with Hans.

Webster's Dictionary defines the verb *function* as "to perform." Teachers and administrators certainly do perform, but no one keeps score. The message of Rule 8 is that when you find yourself in a game where the score is not being kept, build a scoreboard.

In the final analysis, scoring is the source of organizational power. It is not just a nifty thing to do, it is essential for survival. The alternative is to invoke Rule 9. If you can't build a scoreboard, fake it. In the absence of scoring, fans will concentrate on form. If you look good enough, they may not notice that it is all illusion. As you will see in the next chapter, some organizations have survived quite nicely on illusion. Those that didn't made a fatal error: they forgot what was real.

6

Working in Organizations

Where there's a will there's a way.

Famous lawyer

Organizations exist to survive (Rule 6). They are born, they grow, and they die. To understand this life cycle one must consider how organizations come into being. Most companies are started by at least two people: the "outsider," who hustles and innovates; and the "insider," who produces and maintains.

Consider the birth of National Electronics and Telecommunications Operations, Inc. Formed by Conrad Closem and Manfred Makit, the infant company produces pocket-sized computer terminals in an abandoned Amoco station in Secaucus, New Jersey. Conrad gets the orders and Manfred manufactures the units.

In the early years of NEATO's growth, everyone is acutely aware of the need to survive. It's like living in a rowboat with the sea only an arm's length away. With success and prosperity comes increased complexity. There is structure and hierarchy, much of it a result of evolution rather than planning. Perched atop the bridge of the battleship NEATO, Closem and Makit can no longer *directly* control their course. Their concern for survival has greatly diminished. It is illusion, but people begin to believe in the immortality of their structure. The reality is that large organizations, like ships, can and do sink. We may pump them up with air for a while, but only a fool would mistake a balloon for a cannonball.

Take this bizarre example. George was a solid, competent, somewhat autocratic general manager of a small chemical plant. He ran a tight ship and his numbers were always good. In a corporate reorganization, it was decided to use his plant on a part-time basis for other product lines to test new chemicals. At the end of each month, George sent these operations a bill for the use of his facility. They cried "foul," George cried "business," and the net result was George got fired. In his exit interview, George made only one request. He said, "After you turkeys run this place into the ground, I'd like the first opportunity to buy it." Poor George was so intent on moving the ball that he missed the signal that the game had changed.

Life Cycles

Organizations tend to experience four distinct phases in their growth and development. In each, the strategy for success is quite different, as are the risks and payoffs. These are:

Phase	Game	Risk	Payoff
Infancy	"Shooting craps"	High	High
Adolescence	"Pumping iron"	Moderate	High
Maturity	"Milking cows"	Low	Moderate
Old age	"Clipping coupons"	Low	Low

Starting an organization is a high-risk venture. What makes the risk worthwhile is the potential for a big return. Based on bankruptcy records, most fail to survive this phase. The most frequent reason reported is undercapitalization. In gambler's parlance, they came to the table lean and crapped out.

When an organization survives its infancy, the threat of failure lessens while the potential for big payoff remains. Like adolescence, it's a time for building muscle and strength. It is also the most critical phase in the organization's life cycle. Like a weight lifter, it can overextend itself and topple over. The most common cause for failure during this phase is quite simply bad management.

As an organization settles into maturity, it becomes what financial people fondly refer to as a "cash cow." The strategy is to feed and milk it but nothing else. Although it's rare, some organizations manage to fail during this phase, most often because they feed their cows caviar and install wall-to-wall carpeting in the barn.

In the final phase of an organization's life, performance is much like that of a bond. Survival tends to be a function of whether management is content to clip coupons or decides to cash in its chips. Unlike bonds that have a fixed maturation date, organizations can often survive almost indefinitely during this phase. But ultimately they will die, or at least they will cease to exist in their present form. We do not focus on organizational death for morbid reasons but rather to understand how to live and survive; one can learn more about the process function from failure than from success.

When an individual's survival is threatened, it is usually at a time of great stress and change such as the loss of a mate, a new job, or a geographic move. Organizations also experience periods of great stress; these, too, come at times of significant change. Most often they occur during the transition from one phase to the next in the life cycle. In the following sections we will take a brief look at a wide variety of organizations at various stages in their life cycle. The intent is to learn more about process by focusing on content—that is, what kinds of games they are playing and how they are doing. In the absence of any rational order, they will be presented alphabetically.

Airlines

In a flurry of meals, movies, and medicine-show antics, it is easy to forget that the basic business of airlines is to move people and things from one point to another. This kind of forgetfulness accelerated the demise of effective railroad passenger service.

The transportation business is essentially a game of logistics that requires great skill in planning and organizing. In spite of heavy regulation of fares, the range of effectiveness among airlines is as wide as in most other industries. The very cause of failure has been to confuse goals and norms. Extensive regulation and heavy administrative requirements often seduce managers into creating bureaucracies. The nature of a bureaucratic structure is to be brittle and unyielding. Unable to deal with rapid change (oil embargos, DC-10s, and so on) they easily shatter. Consider this firsthand example.

When my wife and I were first married, she worked as a reservations agent for a large airline. A hard-working, conscientious woman, her attendance record was perfect. That winter she caught the flu and was bedridden for two days. As she struggled to get ready for work on the third day, I casually asked what her company's sick-leave policy was. To my amazement, she replied that she would not be paid for the two days. "You have to be out five consecutive days to get paid," she moaned. Incredulous, I pressed further. "Let me see if I've got this straight. If you crawl out of bed and go to work, you are docked for two days. But if you stay in bed for three more days you are paid for all five?" "That's right," she answered. "Well, then, go back to bed. We can't afford for you to go to work," I replied.

Sounds crazy, doesn't it? Not so, if you understand bureaucratic logic. Some corporate whiz kid who couldn't keep his hands off the computer discovered that very few people were ever sick for more than four consecutive days. Thus, a major cost savings was available by simply changing the policy. Of course, it didn't work!

As a postscript, although the airline has changed its sick-leave policy, it continues to lose great sums of money on a regular basis. It survives on cash flow and clipped coupons. But every year its competitors beat it hands down out in the airports of the world.

Part of doing business in corporate America is to be a frequent customer of the airlines. Applying Murphy's Law you will sooner or later experience two unsettling occurrences: lost baggage and missed connections. Notice how the airline deals with these and score them from one to ten. You now have a quick peek into a process whose relationship with financial performance is exceedingly high.

To end on a positive note, my faith in effective management was recently renewed when I had cause to travel on an airline that has a reputation among the regulars as "pit city." Indeed, insiders tell me that a few years ago it was on the very brink of bankruptcy, saved only by the "charity" of the banks (as you will see in the next section, this means that the collateral was worth a fortune).

The plane was delayed due to a mechanical problem. But, atypically, passengers were given a progress report every 15 minutes. Just prior to boarding we were given a brief questionnaire asking, "How did we do during this unfortunate delay?" While this was a very small incident, it should not pass unnoticed that the airline had fairly recently appointed a new president.

Banks

Like airlines, the banking industry is heavily regulated. Here, too, the range of performance has not been limited by regulation. In recent years, one bank actually failed and another was bailed out at the eleventh hour. While the losers bemoan rising interest rates and watch their customers flock to money-market funds, the winners keep on winning. Although obscured on the back pages of financial newspapers, some of these institutions are reporting record earnings.

A case in point was a recent battle among local savings banks for home-improvement-loan business. Bank A had a "sale" and cut its interest rate to 10 percent. Bank B offered a choice of free power tools, advertised heavily, and charged a rate of 13 percent. Astute game players could have predicted the outcome: B won the battle hands down.

The banking industry has awakened to the fact that marketing of services is an active process, not a passive one. It has also begun to learn a lesson learned earlier by department stores. That is, the market is two-tiered; some people want quality and others want convenience. Thus, Bloomingdale's and Neiman Marcus do well, as does K-Mart. But the guy in the middle gets squeezed to death. In the banking business, the quality seeker will never be fooled by pretty prizes or power tools.

Do not be mistaken, however, into thinking that the issue of quality versus convenience is a factor of wealth alone. There are some nice, quiet banks in southern Florida that have an abundance of checking accounts whose average balances are well into six figures. One of their customers was recently quoted as saying, "I don't want any more interest. I wouldn't know what to do with it." If that bank doesn't make house calls, it should.

In the more mundane world of us wage earners, some banks are slowly coming to realize that in spite of all their pomp and circumstance, the name of the game is selling. Major innovations in that business will take place at the point of purchase. Those friendly little neighborhood money stores represent a relatively untapped market. The momentum has already begun with the advent of longer hours, drive-in windows, money machines, and bill paying by telephone. Watch the winners as they try to sing their way into your heart on TV commercials.

Cars

As of this writing, the automobile industry is suffering a severe drop in sales. What many people don't realize is that the automobile business is seasonal and always has been. In this case, however, seasons are marked by economic conditions rather than weather. As with all such enterprises, layoffs abound during the droughts. Unlike fruit picking, however, compensation is handsome during the times of plenty.

The sheer mass of our "big four" makes flexibility and the ability to change a very difficult proposition. Yet each has had its turns at bat. They have had hits, runs, and errors. For some historical perspective, consider these bits of innovative engineering: the Corvette, the Mustang, the Citation, and the Eagle.

The man who fathered the Corvette left GM, wrote a book, and is presently gearing up to manufacture a sports car in Ireland. The major force behind the Mustang was fired from Ford and now runs Chrysler. Even during this time of recession, the demand for Citations and all its front-wheel-drive cousins exceeds production capacity. If there is a market for four-wheel-drive family cars, the AMC Eagle has landed.

The point is that even among these corporate giants, there is still the opportunity for an individual to step up to the plate and hit a home run. At the other extreme, it would be easy merely to kick Chrysler for its horrendous performance and thereby miss some important lessons. First, the organization put its money on the wrong horses; that's an error in judgment, not stupidity. If turbine cars had worked out, they would have been in the driver's seat. (Some puns can't be resisted). Lest we forget, Ford bombed with the Edsel, and GM is sitting on a ton of rotary-engine agreements. Second, if Chrysler can be kept afloat, the man at the helm is the same guy who gave us the Mustang. Damon Runyon once wrote that past performance and breeding will not always predict the winner of a horse race, but that's the way to bet.

Dealerships

"What," you say, "another section on cars?" Not quite. Automobile dealerships are *not* in the car business! Consider this: a very small percentage of a dealer's sales force accounts for the majority of sales. Further, these "heavy hitters" are a fickle lot and often move from place to place with little loyalty to any particular make. But they do equally well regardless of the name on the fender. A dealership is a *store* and its business is retailing. Just to make it interesting, most are required to carry only one brand.

Judging by the number of dealerships that fail and the fact that most are oblivious to the heavy-hitter phenomenon, they tend to be among the worst-run businesses. Perhaps they are blinded by all that polished chrome and sleek enamel. In any event they are in serious need of Rule 10.

> *Rule 10:* Organizations fail when they don't know what business they are in.

A dealership is a *store,* sports fans! Once that four-wheeled goody hits the floor it belongs to the dealer. The manufacturer has closed its sale; now it's up to our hero, the storekeeper, to finance it, polish it, and sell it. To do so you need a sales force—a real one, not six unemployed prune farmers and a retired yak breeder. It also helps if you have a sales manager, one who can plan, organize, direct, and control those little devils who keep trying to sell the gas tank as a dealer-installed option.

As mentioned in the previous section, auto sales are a bit soft right now. (That's sales slang for "stinks.") But some dealerships are booming. Some particularly clever ones have obtained the right to sell a number of different makes and sell them all under one roof. Presto—the supermarket has been reinvented. Also, it's a pretty good strategy for attracting and keeping those all important sales stars.

Electric Companies

It is paradoxical that, in terms of process, organizations that sell power appear to have very little. Caught between the energy crunch, consumerists, antinuclear activists, and price controls, power is not a business any sane person would enter freely. Power companies are stuck milking cows that are running dry and clipping coupons whose value is ever diminishing. Even the widows and orphans have abandoned them.

As luck would have it, I live just north of the boundary between my city's public utility and a power co-op. On any given month my co-op neighbors to the south pay about 25 percent of what I do for the same amount of electricity. Since the city outfit has not been reporting huge profits, I can only assume that one bet right and the other bet wrong—assuming, of course, that there was once a time where a choice was possible.

It is difficult to say just what business the utilities are in. The deck is very much stacked against them. It certainly isn't the energy business; perhaps it's the political business.

As in all games, there are exceptions. A recent newspaper article reported that a Florida utility discovered it could buy coal from Poland and have it delivered for half the price of U.S. coal. To add insult to injury, the Polish coal was less polluting than the American product. Of course, there was considerable rhetoric as the coal companies blamed high rail costs and the railroads blamed cheap overseas labor for the price difference. All of which is irrelevant to the fact that a knowledgeable player joined the game.

Factories

As was mentioned in a previous chapter, the dilemma of working in a factory is that it was designed for machines not people. Failure, however, is almost entirely a function of performance. Consider the following case.

The Wellington Widget Works has established that the standard of excellence for widget welders is 100 units per eight-hour day. Brian Brash, a young newcomer to the organization, consistently welds 150 units in seven hours. Unfortunately he is often late to work and occasionally leaves early. After repeated warnings, he is fired. At the same time, Melvin Mediocre produces 90 units per day. Melvin has been employed by Wellington for nearly 20 years.

His supervisor gave up trying to improve Mel's performance a long time ago.

Factories hang on the horns of a difficult dilemma. By design they are created to perform perfectly. They are like a big black box in which raw materials go in one end and finished product comes out the other. Imperfect performance is due to human error. Thus, a factory is a constant source of punishment rather than reward.

The secret of effective factory management is to *insulate* people from the impersonal demands of the mechanical process and to create instead the opportunity to be rewarded for less-than-perfect achievement. By tolerating a bit of brashness, rather than settling for a sea of mediocrity, volume will go up and costs will go down. In the end, that is what the factory game is all about.

Gas Stations

In 1971 my local pump proprietor enticed me to "fill it up" with offers of steak knives, game cards, and Green Stamps. In 1974 he rewarded a two-hour predawn wait by dribbling in $3.00 worth. Last month he could not sell his full allotment of gasoline.

Unlike many of his colleagues, my still friendly neighborhood fuel merchant was not beaten by the whipsaw of international oil games. He had figured out a long time ago that he didn't want to be in the gas business. Instead, he put all his emphasis on repair work. His bays are always filled and three tow trucks stand at the ready. He provides prompt efficient service; he even picks up and delivers.

Hospitals

Health care is a serious business; it is also a very expensive one. The major barriers to understanding health-care organizations are the medical mystique and the involvement of third-party payment (medical insurance). The impact of these barriers is to create confusion between two separate and distinct goals. The medical business aims to provide quality health care. The hospital business attempts to run a facility at maximum efficiency. These goals do not always coincide. Indeed, at times they are in direct conflict.

The bottom line in the hospital business is occupancy rate. Fill all the beds and the P&L will take care of itself—sometimes. Run with half your beds empty and the red ink will flow—always.

The hospital dilemma is that at the crassest level it is a business that is highly dependent on outside contractors (the physicians) to provide service. This often results in a power struggle over who is running which business.

Several solutions have been developed to resolve this dilemma, and they appear to be working. First came health centers in which all staff were full-time members with little or no outside loyalties to an independent practice. By combining the medical business with the hospital business, significant increases in effectiveness were made possible.

A second strategy was the combination of several hospitals into a single corporate unit. This generates such obvious benefits as combined purchasing power and centralized billing, but a much more significant—though rather subtle—payoff is the increased control over the patient population (the marketplace) and thus a reduction in the ability of individual physicians to run the hospital. A case in point went as follows.

Dr. Ossie T. Pathic ran the finest orthopedic unit in the city. When Monongahela General refused to buy him a new piece of equipment, he traveled across town to see the head of Susquehanna Sanitarium. "Buy me an atomic flitwaddle ($1.2 million, retail) and I'll transfer my operation to your hospital," he propositioned. Unfortunately for Dr. Pathic, Monongahela was part of a corporate complex that wielded so much power that Susquehanna was unwilling to risk accusations of medical piracy. It blew the whistle on Ossie.

Should I ever need the services of a doctor who has read this book, I should point out that none of the above is meant as a condemnation of physicians. They are human; their loyalty is to their patients, their profession, and their practice. Applying Rule 1, they will act in those interests before considering the needs of a hospital. To paraphrase an old soldier's lament, running a hospital is too important a business to be left in the hands of physicians.

Insurance

It is said of backgammon that it takes minutes to learn and a lifetime to master. The life-insurance game also seems much simpler on the surface than it is in reality. Consider this; the failure rate for first-year salespeople is 85 percent. Further, most of the dollar sales volume is attributable to 10 percent of the people employed.

As any good gambler knows, a high-risk situation can be very attractive if the potential payoff is equally high. One has only to peruse a few insurance-company balance sheets to see that the pay-off is indeed attractive.

If ever there were a business that paid great attention to score-keeping, it is insurance. On an actuarial basis there are none better. However, the ability to keep score bears no relationship to the ability to sell a policy any more than memorizing probability tables will ensure winning a hand of poker. The insurance game is a selling business, perhaps the most difficult because the item sold is intangible. Indeed, on a logical basis, life insurance is one of the few things we buy that we hope we will never use. To sell *that* requires deep insight into Rule 11.

> *Rule 11:* People do not behave logically; they behave psychologically.

A recent series of television commercials depicts the pathos of surviving families whose breadwinner was not sufficiently insured. The message was clearly aimed to push the "guilt button" of those who profess to have as their highest priority the welfare of their family. If such were truly the case, there would be no need to "sell" the idea.

If altruism were the motive of such commercials, they would also point out that term insurance is far superior to whole life and that some of the least expensive rates are charged by savings banks.

The reality of the situation is that whole life is pushed because it is most profitable for the company and the salesperson. As an investment it is one of the worst, second only to U.S. Savings Bonds. That is the logic. The "psychologic" is that we buy our insurance from good old Fred and painlessly buy bonds through payroll deductions where we work.

Japanese Business

Mine is perhaps the last generation that will remember the phrase "made in Japan" as a euphemism for poor quality. Since the end of World War II the chips have piled up on the Asian end of the international gaming table at an astounding rate. From automobiles to stereos, the competitiveness of their products with regard to quality and price has "tapped out" many a U.S. player. While much can be learned from the content side of this phenomenon, as always the real secrets lie in the process. The way to learn a game is to watch the cards, the way to master it is to watch the play. Consider these two "hands."

When U.S. businessmen were negotiating with Japan for distribution rights for transistor radios, they noticed a curious thing. On what seemed like random occasions the Japanese would adjourn to meet by themselves. With chuckles of superiority, it was concluded that our new allies were stuck with a cumbersome process of decision making. The end result, however, put an interesting twist on proceedings. When the Japanese returned to the bargaining table they brought with them a proposition that probably sounded something like this: "After much discussion, we have concluded that the real issue is not one of transistor radios but rather of distribution. Thus, we would like to arrange for *all* our products to be sold in your country." Now it was the Americans' turn to call for an adjournment, as such a request went beyond their authority. The rest, as they say, is history. It was teamwork, not technology, that turned the trick.

In Chapter 4, the productivity dilemma as it relates to labor costs was explored. In the United States, such costs have been skyrocketing while productivity increases have been marginal, to say the least. In the past, some organizations have tried to pull an ace out of their sleeve through automation. Although such technology has been around for decades, its use has been greatly limited. Promises of productivity increases have not generally been realized. But that may be changing. Industry is starting to get very interested in the use of robots. What is most significant is that over half of the world's robots are in Japanese factories! To add insult to injury, those little items are *not* being exported.

Kola

Looks funny spelled that way, doesn't it? Such is the power of advertising. From aspirin to corn flakes the name of the game is brand loyalty. The soft-drink industry is a prime example.

Consider the case of Dr. Pepper. In the past decade it has doubled its share of the soft-drink market, tripled sales, and quintupled earnings—in spite of a recent quote by its CEO, who said, "We've never known how to tell you what it tastes like, plus our name doesn't mean anything. If you line up ten people who have never had it and don't say what it is, nine of them won't like it."

In some ways the pop business is like the car business. Just as auto manufacturers sell to dealers, soda producers sell to bottlers. Unlike the dealer, however, the bottler is a classic example of the "middle man" who neither produces the product nor sells to the user. While the automobile supermarket is very much the exception in its field, bottlers are free to carry whatever brands they choose.

As a result, the soft-drink business is really two separate but related businesses: production and bottling. The common thread is the expectation of brand loyalty. Blind taste tests have consistently proved that most people can't tell the difference between Coke, Pepsi, and Brand X. With their names visible, however, the unpopular brands will gather dust, regardless of the price. Thus, the risks for the producer are enormous, but so are the rewards, as exemplified by Dr. Pepper's performance. The soft-drink game is a monumental crapshoot reserved for high rollers. Judging by the number of new products that come and go, there is apparently no shortage of players.

Laundry

The fragile mortality of business is clearly demonstrated by the recent history of the laundry and dry cleaning industry. The introduction and proliferation of permanent-press fabrics caused many to go under fast. Those that survived have done so through sound management and some luck.

A case that was much more skill than luck was Loeb's Laundry and Dry Cleaners, which was collapsing due to a shrinking market. A new president was brought in by the aging founder, and when this somewhat brash young man looked at the business, he was able to see the forest as well as the trees. What he saw was:

1. a dry cleaning plant
2. a fleet of trucks
3. a loyal, experienced work force
4. a bevy of old stores in deteriorating neighborhoods

As a student of Rule 10, the new president turned that knowledge to his advantage. Essentially he said to himself, "Given these resources, what business should I be in?" His answer marked Loeb's entry into the uniform-rental business. Recognizing that a large number of companies provide work clothes for their employees, he set about selling them on renting from him. This plan made use of the first three resources on his list and allowed him to divest Loeb's of many stores that were in need of retirement. Today sales and profits are at an all-time high. There are problems, of course, but they are problems of growth rather than of stagnation—pumping iron, not milking cows (or, in this case, kicking a dead horse).

Motels

The motel was once a marvelous innovation that combined the need for temporary living space with the increasing use of automobiles. Indeed, the lodging business continues to reflect both the growth and change of our society. As with many other industries, such growth has required the skilled game player to look around to see if Rule 10 was gaining on him or her.

A constant complaint of most people who travel on business is that of poor service. As one traveler pointed out, "I want a fast newspaper, a fast breakfast, and a fast check-out." In fact, these needs first prompted the proliferation of motels. But many motels got greedy and forgot what business they were in. Rapid growth produced structures that were motels in name only. Rising high into the skyline, these complexes found themselves in businesses ranging from boutiques to gourmet restaurants to swinging singles' spots.

In direct contrast to the individual traveler's needs are the wide range of services required by a convention or conference. Anyone who has ever had the opportunity to administer one of these logistical nightmares can attest to the fact that Murphy's Law is alive and well. One answer has been the development of "conference centers." Built specifically for conferences and conventions, they are a far cry from the Quick Courts Motels that dot the nation's highways. The only problem, and a delightful one for the owners, is that organizations gobble up the available space so quickly that it is difficult to attract new business without the risk of further expansion. They are further proof that winners are invariably very clear about what game they are in.

Nonprofit Organizations

Perhaps the greatest barrier to achieving excellence in a not-for-profit organization is the expectation that effective management is not possible. Saddled with the usual committee structure, they often cling to survival by their fingernails.

As a sometime consultant to these organizations, my highest priority has been to teach Rule 10. My experience has been that as a group these organizations do not define what business they are in. The major barrier to self-definition appears to be a great herd of sacred cows. Indeed, in religious organizations one such bovine is the mythical aura of power attributed to the leader. Such power is, according to my rabbinical and clerical friends, not so much mythical as nonexistent. The power, they say, is clearly on the board, not the pulpit.

In *Fiddler on the Roof*, Tevya bemoans the fact that people no longer pay homage to tradition. Faced with a world that continues to change without his permission, he sings of his frustration. As a content variable, tradition is a marvelously comforting value that reinforces the norms of stability and survival. As a process variable, however, it can be a death trap. As society changes, so must the institutions that support it. Those that don't will cease to exist.

The Federal Tax Code recognizes at least 26 separate categories of tax-exempt organizations. The IRS tends to see its relationship with these operations as contractual. Such organizations are required to detail specifically what they will do and how they will operate before they receive the government's blessing and reduced postal rates. Although it wasn't the government's intent, such a process is a beautiful example of Rule 10 in action. It just may reduce the number of failures among those organizations that meet the government's criteria.

Orthodonists

Picture a circle of dental chairs facing inward. Attached to the arm of each chair is a metal "flag" not unlike that found on a mailbox. Printed on this flag are the words "Ready for Dentist." The assembly line has come to dental medicine. A fantasy? No, as any parent of a crooked-tooth teenager will be quick to tell you.

The fee-for-service business continues to fight the dilemma of limited assets. Dentists have been in the forefront of this battle by delegating and routinizing as much as possible. The importance of this process goes far beyond the dental profession. As the service sector of the economy grows to an ever increasing share of the marketplace, so will the needs for effective management and productive results. The path is clear for independent professionals such as doctors, lawyers, and accountants, but much less has been done by in-house practitioners and corporate staff people to control their own destiny. Removed from the day-to-day concern for profitability, their security and "survivability" rest in the hands of others. The net result is an environment that is ruled by something between paternalism and politics.

Astute game players should quickly recognize that the process issue is one of score keeping, or more precisely the lack thereof. Without such measurement, norms and values take the place of goals and objectives. Being a good soldier becomes more important than winning the war.

Much has been written about politics and paternalism in organizations. At first blush they would appear to be direct opposites. In reality, company stores and corporate infighting are but two examples of individuals and groups reacting to an imbalance of power. The name of the game is still survival, but without a direct link to business results, the organization invariably loses. All its energy is devoted to keeping afloat and none is left to move it forward. Emphasis is placed on style rather than results. This is the essence of Rule 12.

√ *Rule 12:* When goals are not measurable, form replaces
function.

Some corporate staffers have awakened to the fact that re-arranging deck chairs on the *Titanic* is a poor strategy for survival no matter how well they perform it. Their creation of staff "profit centers" has been a giant step toward improving that situation. If the service will sell on the open market, it will sell in-house as well. They have stumbled onto Rule 13.

Rule 13: All goals are measurable.

Postal Service

Once upon a time a group of graduate students in search of thesis material were given permission to study a post office. As luck would have it, their professor was a measurement buff who insisted on numerical documentation. Poring over performance data, the students uncovered a startling comparison. The mail-sorting crew on the night shift produced three times the output of the other crews. The sorting task itself was fairly straightforward. Each worker sat in front of a matrix of pigeonholes labeled by zip code. Sacks of mail were sorted by placing letters in the appropriate slot. Skill level alone would not account for the difference in output, although spot checks revealed they excelled in accuracy as well. The students decided to investigate further.

The night crew arrived promptly and bantered easily with each other. Just before starting time, a glass dish was placed in the center of the room. Reaching for pockets and purses, each crew member dropped in a quarter and quickly proceeded to sorting. Twenty minutes later one of the workers jumped up and exclaimed, "Got it!" She then emptied the dish of coins, leaving only one behind. The others crowded around her sorting bin briefly and then reached for another quarter. Throughout the shift this behavior was repeated over and over again with different crew members "getting it."

What was going on? Quite simply, they were playing bingo! The first worker to fill a line of slots—horizontally, vertically, or diagonally—won the contents of the dish. With their own money, these people had found a way to make a boring job fun, and in the process they improved the quantity and quality of their work. (The penalty for cheating was to be banned from playing.)

If this were an old-fashioned fairy tale, everyone would live happily ever after and march into the sunset humming a few bars from Rule 13. Unfortunately, since the postal supervisors could not take credit for the amazing performance improvement, they invoked Rule 12. The night shift was chastised for gambling and the games were ended. Quite predictably, performance returned to "normal."

Quickies and Quality

Fast-food franchises have been a phenomenon of the last decade that once again proves the power of Rule 10. Quickness alone cannot explain the success of these burger parlors and chicken shops. Diners and cafés with equally speedy service have been around for more than a century. What is different is sharp focus, structure, and high quality.

Sharp focus means a clearly defined market. Such definition includes customers, product, and location. McDonald's places great emphasis on children, while Wendy's appears to go after the adults. This focus is reinforced by advertising, décor, and food selections. Indeed, a tremendous amount of research is done before an item is added to the menu. Equally intensive research is conducted to determine site selection.

Singleness of purpose is further reinforced by rigidly controlled store layouts. Having worked through problems of what goes where, franchises are not encouraged to be creative. Indeed there are severe penalties for abandoning the system. This is not done for altruistic reasons, nor from a desire for perfect order. Rather, the motive is the clear recognition that each carefully cloned cousin represents the rest of the family. A bad experience in one can quickly sour a customer on all.

The watchword of the fast-food restaurant business is that you are only as good as your last meal. The quality control that the more successful fast-food franchises place on their products borders on the fanatical. Their criteria for acceptable ground beef could not be met by the fussiest supermarket.

Such are the lyrics of the fast-food business. Like a laser beam, they have cut a path of success through one of the riskiest terrains in the marketplace. The content aspects of short menus, tight control, and cookie-cutter construction have certainly played a significant part in their success. But there is important music to be heard as well.

The care and feeding of teenage employees has not escaped the practiced eye of the founding franchisors. Values of loyalty, hard work, punctuality, and cleanliness are delivered in an almost cult-like atmosphere. These values have an impact not only on the employees but on the customers as well. Notice how few diners leave these establishments without disposing of their own trash. You will not find such behavior in Bert's Beanery. Nor will you find it among the many losers who tried to copy the words but never heard the music. Unlike horseshoes, close does not count.

Restaurants

A few years ago a small French restaurant opened. It prepared a marvelous array of food that would tantalize the palate of the most discriminating gourmet. Located in a charming, renovated building, dinner was an experience that lasted close to three hours. Over time, several changes were made: first, a large bar was added; second, service was significantly speeded up; third, the quality of food diminished.

From the consumer's viewpoint, these changes were sad. From the businessperson's, they were understandable. The profit margin on alcoholic beverages is so great that it makes food preparation no more than a "loss-leader." Since the name of the game is booze not bread, it pays handsomely to "turn over" a table as often as possible during dining hours. Finally, since food is overhead rather than a profit producer, cost reductions can be made at the expense of quality—particularly when the majority of one's customers don't differentiate between exceptional and better-than-average taste. Indeed, if the liquor really moves, it may be questionable whether anyone *can* detect a difference.

As was mentioned in the previous section on fast-food franchises, restaurants live and die by their last meal. It only takes one bad experience to lose a steady customer forever. But do not take the term "meal" literally. People frequent restaurants for a whole host of reasons, most of which have nothing to do with food; the restaurant business is built on Rule 11 (people do not behave logically . . .).

The failure rate of restaurants is very high, not just for the newcomers, but even for the old, established places. It is as if such businesses never mature beyond the adolescent phase, with high risk constantly lurking around every corner. The essential reason for this continual risk is that in many ways they are the antithesis of the fast-food establishments. In place of having a sharp focus, they often attempt to be all things to all people. They may hit a hot streak and become the "in" spot. Just as quickly, they can become forgotten.

As of this writing, that small French restaurant is hanging on— barely. To its right is a beef-and-bird place that is currently the hot singles' "watering hole." To its left is a new restaurant—the third try in that spot in less than two years.

There is an attraction to the restaurant business that goes far beyond its limited potential to make a big buck. Indeed, on a logical basis there is little to recommend the almost daily crapshoot of trying to guess how many customers will show up and what they will choose to order. Copying a page from the fast-food handbook, some have gone the route of very limited menus. Since we have already established that groceries don't pay the bills, such a strategy would appear well founded.

Supermarkets

The grocery business is a prime example of a zero-sum game. In other words, in order for one player to win some amount (money or market share, for example), another player must lose an equivalent amount. Like a table-stakes poker game, it is assumed that everything is on the table. In business games, this is called a mature market. Another aspect to the grocery game is that no major player possesses a substantial advantage over the others in terms of resources. As in most high-stakes poker games, the net result is that there are rarely more than two players left when it comes time to count up the chips. The dynamics of this process are at the heart of gaming theory and have important implications for managers, particularly those who are charged with directing the destiny of their business. The old saw "Two's company and three's a crowd" stands on an astute process observation.

To get down to particulars, whenever a third person or organization enters the game, a new option opens up in terms of competition. Prior to the third participant's entry the two original players (market leaders) have learned to coexist with large shares of market; examples of this include Coke and Pepsi, Budweiser and Miller, GM and Ford. A new guy on the block is a threat to both, and one may discover that they collude to prevent him from succeeding. This is summarized in Rule 14.

Rule 14: Three into two won't go.

Barring major technological innovations (diet soda, light beer, front-wheel drive), price will not determine the outcome of this game; indeed, "price wars" rarely accomplish anything when only two players are in the game. However, it *is* an effective strategy for squeezing out a brash (and hopefully undercapitalized) new competitor.

The beauty of the supermarket game is that it comes closest to being purely zero-sum. Both carry the same products and serve the same markets. The price changes, games, and gimmicks of one can be equaled by the competition—and often are within days. The only difference that remains is skill—*management skill*. In this case, the astute player knows that in spite of all the publicity to the contrary, the bulk of grocery shoppers are *not* price conscious; they will go for convenience every time. Here then is the box score of one such game recently played.

Stag and Wigwam had emerged decades ago as the two major supermarkets in a geographic area and controlled well over 90 percent of the market. Location is critical to such ventures (the convenience factor), and both were well placed. Most often they had stores across the street from each other. A number of chains had made a run at them but fell short. One such operation that had not entered their market had a "friendly" agreement with Wigwam to stay in its own territory thirty miles away in exchange for a similar freedom from competition in its home base.

But times were changing. As the suburbs pushed eastward into previously rural areas, space was quietly purchased by the "friendly" outsider. With what appeared to be an economic *blitzkrieg*, the new chain made its move by opening five stores at once, all located in key spots serving the new suburbia. Backed by strong advertising, friendly service, and well-appointed stores, the newcomer came to play and came to stay. It appears to be doing very well.

At first glance this anecdote may appear to contradict Rule 14. But look closer. Recall that the friendly agreement was between Wigwam and the newcomer; Stag was not involved. Further investigation reveals that while Wigwam has been building new stores and refurbishing old ones, Stag has not. Finally, the five newcomer's stores are located across from the few Stag markets that do not have Wigwam stores directly opposite. Can you smell the coffee?

Television

The most visual evidence of Rule 14 is the television broadcasting business. At times there is more excitement behind the screens than on the tube. Unlike supermarkets, the opportunity for product differentiation in television is huge. The fact that programs appear bland and similar points out the power of Rule 15.

> *Rule 15:* When you are winning, don't change the game.

Innovation is rarely generated by market leaders. Having overcome the high risks during the crap-shooting phase, networks appear compelled to ride with their winners and quickly cut their losers, which may explain why there is so much imitation on TV. The only sure way to determine when a winner has become a loser is to ride it into the ground. While guaranteeing that you will be sure when you have really lost, this procedure also guarantees that you will have losers. But as any successful gambler will tell you, the secret to going home healthy is to quit a winner.

While the essence of Rule 15 is deceptively simple, its corollary is not. The other side of the coin is Rule 16.

> *Rule 16:* When the odds are against you, change the game.

The success of Atlanta's "superstation" has been based on this notion. Rather than compete head-on with the major networks, it has carved out an alternative market using satellite technology to extend its range beyond the borders of Georgia.

A similar situation exists for cable television. Although off to a rather rocky start, it has a high likelihood of success because the market is there. As with most new concepts, the technology already exists but awaits the management skill to make it work. Concepts do not define the rules; the players do. Indeed, the most common sign that the game has changed is the entry of a new player.

Universities

What could be a clearer and more straightforward business than academe—the hallowed halls of ivy? Alas, colleges and universities have also found themselves driven aground on the rocky shores of Rule 10. Many have discovered that the result of not knowing what business they were in resulted in their inability to survive. Like banks, hospitals, and other prestigious institutions, form replaced function (Rule 12).

The central dilemma of universities is that tuition and fees do not fully cover operating expenses. Burdened with huge overhead, donations and investments have not kept pace with inflation. Add declining enrollments, and the game gets exceedingly tough.

The business of higher education has never been a gentleman's game. Beneath its prim, academic exterior the political infighting can get quite bloody. Consider the often discussed dynamic of "publish or perish." While outwardly extolling the virtues of teaching, the *game value* of the professor is his or her ability to attract grants. Such grants are a major source of revenue because they ease the painful burden of expenses somewhat.

It is unfortunate but true that teaching ability does not carry any weight in the marketplace. Rare is the student who picks a college on the basis of who is in residence. On the other hand, *overall* academic excellence will affect a university's ability to attract students in the longer run. Those institutions that live on the knife's edge of survival must perform a delicate balancing act.

The preceding observation is based on the assumption that a university has chosen, willingly or unwillingly, to play its game within the confines of academia. But it has an alternative—the sports business. The combination of gate receipts, television fees, and national publicity provides handsome payoffs far in excess of those available through traditional academic channels. In the past decade only one new university has entered the game with any major success. It should be noted that it fielded a basketball team that often makes the national top-ten list.

Recently, Stanford University added a new twist. Committed to playing the academic game, it wrestled with the dilemma of attracting fresh talent to a part of the country where housing costs are unaffordable for anyone without independent means or fat equity. Stanford's solution was to offer to pick up a major part of the cost of buying homes for faculty members. The "kicker" is that when a house is sold, the university gets a proportioned share of the capital gains. Thus, in one bold move it has given itself an edge in attracting talent *and* has created a new source of income.

Valet Parking

It was a bitterly cold day when I landed at the airport. Recent snowfall had put twelve inches on the ground. In the long-term parking lot, plows had cleared the lanes and piled ten-foot drifts over the cars in the process. Thus, it was with great delight that I spotted a tow truck idling in the lot. My enthusiasm quickly turned to anger after the following dialogue: "Can you please pull my car out?" I asked. "It'll cost you 20 bucks, Mac," replied the driver. "Do you have a shovel I can borrow?" I tried. "Nope," he answered. Warmed by wrath and adrenaline, I cleared my car barehanded and drove off an hour later.

A few days later I learned from a friend that one of the smaller auto-rental firms located across the street from the airport had begun a valet-parking service. Although the word "valet" suggested a stiff price, my recent experience encouraged me to try it. Here is what I discovered:

1. The price was exactly the same as the long-term parking lot's.
2. I was driven to and from the rental lot.
3. When I called for my car, I found it had been brushed clean of snow, with the motor running and the heater on.
4. My claim check even had a dime taped to it to make the phone call!

Once again, we have evidence of a master game player at work. But there remained a curious omission. Why did the owner not advertise this marvelous service? Surely he was not content to rely on word of mouth to promote his new business.

The answer came six months later. The county that owned and operated the airport (*and* its parking lots) went to court to prevent valet-parking services from picking up or discharging passengers at the airport. The airport lost that battle. Although never mentioned, the fact that our hero kept a low profile proved to be a major factor in that decision.

Washington

Our government continues to be a favorite target for professional and amateur criticism. Given its cumbersome structure and great visibility, it provides a never-ending supply of material for journalists, commentators, and stand-up comedians. One has only to read the marvelous wit of Will Rogers to realize that the *form* of the game has remained relatively unchanged. Indeed, the process of government is an almost perfect example of Rule 12. In spite of all the polls, promises, and percentages, there is no real measurement of performance.

Xerography

A sure way to get an "edge" in a game is to create a new one. While this doesn't guarantee success, it does create favorable odds. Such is the promise of technology. One such promise that has been handsomely fulfilled is the success of Xerox Corporation.

The problem with an edge is that it dulls. As other players join the game, some learn to play it very well, perhaps even better than the originator. In the case of photocopying, some newcomers have proved to be students of Rule 16. Competition involved, not only new players, but changes in the game as well. With a significant market share, Xerox was content to lease its copiers. Many of the newcomers, however, sold their machines outright. This caused Xerox some embarrassment as many of their machines were not competitively priced. The result, albeit a tad late, was that Xerox cut purchase prices by as much as 20 to 30 percent. But now they are playing the competition's game.

Yankees

If ever there was a game that was heavy on measurement it is the great old American pastime of baseball. Even before the age of the computer, much focus was put on such minutiae as which left-hander had the most strike-outs on a rainy Wednesday. In spite of these statistics, which added to the mystique of the game in days of yore, the business side of baseball is guilty of much befuddlement.

Books like *Ball Four* and *The Bronx Zoo* have removed much of the mystique, but the confusion remains. Why, for example, does Billy Martin keep getting fired when his track record is nothing less than spectacular?

The answer, perhaps, is that the owners confuse two games: baseball the sport and baseball the business. As a for-profit enter-prise, baseball is show biz where the box office is what counts. Only as a pure sport does the box score carry full weight. There is a connection, of course. A winning team "usually" draws crowds while a losing one often suffers through poor attendance and red ink. When owners focus on the wrong box—that is, if they mean busi-ness—they ultimately suffer for it. Many, it would seem, are merely indulging themselves in a hobby—a very expensive one, particu-larly when played poorly.

Zippers, Zippos, and Razor Blades

Long ago and far away the name *Zipper* was a trademark for a product that revolutionized the garment business. Like *Jell-O,*

Kleenex, and *Xerox* it is a brand name that slowly became a generic term for the product itself. The marketing folks did such a splendid job of creating instant brand identification that the legal departments were left with the impossible task of reversing it once fame and fortune were achieved. As a most ludicrous example, can you imagine a patron in a restaurant ordering "Sanka Brand Decaffeinated Coffee"?

The game of brand loyalty, like all games, has a beginning, a middle, and an end. As most tournament players will tell you, the end game is a most crucial and not-to-be-ignored phase. One can indeed win the battles and lose the war. Creating a new product or service is a prime example of not playing the other man's game. However, once the game has begun or the patent runs out, consumer loyalty may be replaced by "what-have-you-done-for-me-lately?"

A prime example is the shaving business. Just when I get used to the latest blade, a new, improved version is introduced. In search of the perfect shave, I eventually try it. Naturally, it doesn't fit the old handle. It is interesting to note that the original marketing strategy was to give away the razor and make a profit on the blades. This strategy has come full circle, with most of the hardware now built into the blade. Indeed, such an evolution laid the groundwork for disposable razors.

While the above discussion has interesting content value for marketing folks, the process lessons are equally rewarding. By continuing to change the game, the market leaders stay one jump ahead of the competition.

At the other extreme is the fate of the Zippo lighter. A product of unquestioned quality, it could not withstand the market attack by disposable lighters. In one fell swoop, a bit of technology did away with flint, fluid, and fuss. How swiftly one game ends and another begins.

PART III

PRODUCTIVITY

Man does not live by bread alone.

Famous nutritionist

7

Performance

I know the game is crooked but it's the only one in town.

Famous loser

As a child, my first exposure to the concept of work was the fable of the ant and the grasshopper. While the grasshopper fiddled his summer away, the ant labored to gather food for the long, cold winter ahead. Proper justice was served when, in the end, the foolish grasshopper starved to death and the ant survived. In adult books this fable is retold as the Protestant Work Ethic.

The problem with such fables is they are all black and white. There is little room for subtle grays. Even as a child, I wondered why the ant didn't trade some food and shelter for a winter of fine violin music.

One real value of fables is to reinforce a simple truth, "Things ain't always what they seem." They also reinforce the basic honesty of children. It was, after all, a child who spoke up when the naked emperor pranced down the street in his new "robe."

The fundamentals of management from my perspective are what I call the three M's: money, motivation, and Mother Goose. The importance of the last category is the essential need for seeing things the way they really are. Mother Goose was an important management theorist, even if she didn't know it. That's why children make marvelous consultants. Consider the eight-year-old who asked his mother why Daddy brought work home from the office every night. Her adult answer was, "Because he didn't have time to finish it at the office." The child's response was quick and to the point, "Well, why don't they put him in a slower class?"

What keeps a management consultant in business is his or her ability to help a client see the world with childlike clarity and to apply the wisdom of Maslow, McGregor, Machiavelli, and Mother G. Remember the goose that laid the golden egg? She was killed in an effort to increase productivity. The same thing happens in industry. We fool around with money, blow smoke about motivation, and end up cooking our own goose.

Money

Let's talk about money. I'm sure you have read that money does not motivate people to work harder or more effectively. I'm just as sure you don't believe a word of it.

Money is a marvelous instrument for recognizing and creating competent performance. That's the good news. It is an equally powerful incentive for incompetence. That's the bad news. You need a clear eye to see which is happening. If you are not getting the performance you want from people, there is a 90 percent probability that you are rewarding a lower level of performance.

Here are a couple of examples. Salespeople are not bringing in new business that is vital to your company's growth. You give pep talk after pep talk and get no visible results. Look at your incentive system from a salesperson's point of view. A call on an old customer is greeted warmly and has a high likelihood of repeat business. A cold call, on the other hand, offers high risk, possible rejection, and the same commission rate as the warm call. There is no incentive for new business.

Or take sick-leave policy. You give ten days paid sick leave. If employees don't use it, they lose it. Everybody takes it. All of it. There is no incentive not to. Want to reduce sick leave taken? Pay people for each day left at the end of the year. Sick leave would drop precipitously.

My favorite story about money is attributed to George Bernard Shaw. He is reputed to have turned to a dinner companion and asked, "Madam, would you go to bed with a stranger for $1 million?" After some thought she replied, "Yes, I would." "Would you do the same for $2?" he inquired. "Of course not," she replied with righteous indignation. "What kind of woman do you think I am?" Shaw quickly responded, "Madam, we have already established *that;* we are merely haggling price."

Motivation

Let's turn our attention to an adult fairy tale. Call it the Myth of Management and Motivation. It goes something like this: When employees do not perform well or are absent a lot, they are presumed to be unmotivated. They are then threatened to shape up or ship out. If their behavior changes, it is assumed they have been motivated. Harry Levinson, the Harvard psychologist, calls this the "Great Jackass Fallacy." With a carrot in one hand and a stick in the other, you make donkeys out of your employees.

An equivalent fairy tale deals with the professor and the frog. Standing before her attentive class, the professor demonstrates that every time she says, "Jump," the frog leaps across her desk. Then with two deft slashes of her scalpel she hamstrings the poor creature. Now when she says, "Jump," the frog remains motionless. "You see, class," she explains, "Without the hamstring muscle the frog is deaf."

This same nonsensical logic is applied to people and motivation. So, without further ado, let's take a clear-eyed look at this whole business. It has been over 50 years since behavioral scientists first gave us the fundamental truth about why people act the way they do. There is a stimulus, and there is a response. If the stimulus is a need such as hunger and the response, such as food, satisfies that need, the two become connected or reinforced. The next time that need arises, the response will be almost automatic.

Now what, you may ask, does this have to do with people and performance? Perhaps a great deal. It means that there are two critical and equally important aspects of motivation. First, there are motives (stimuli); and second, there are incentives (responses). In other words, no matter how hungry people are for the rewards that performance promises, they will not perform if these rewards are not given. Also, no matter how delicious the rewards may seem to others, performance will not improve if the performer is not hungry.

There are two different ways to increase the motivation to perform. One way is to create motives. That's what that large fruit company did when it discovered that pickers would stay in the fields only until they earned enough to fill their pantries with food. In a more modern setting, a company in Baltimore put a lottery ticket in the pay envelopes of those employees who worked a full five-day week. Absenteeism dropped significantly.

An alternative approach is to provide incentives. Remember, an incentive is a response that satisfies a motive. If the motive is not there, the incentive is not really an incentive. Thus, you can talk about the importance of working overtime to a group of young, single employees until you are blue in the face. The fact of the matter is that time and a half on Saturday night is no substitute for Disco Fever.

Money Again

We now come crashing into what seems like a contradiction. There are two kinds of incentives: money and strokes. Strokes are pats on the back, recognition for good work, trophies, and medals. But when push comes to shove, *money is potentially the most powerful incentive*. The kicker is the word "potentially"; the potential remains untapped. The reasons money has not fulfilled its promise are many and complex. Simply put, if monetary incentives were paid out on the basis of competence, many high-income people would have to change their life style. Their fear "corks up" the potential of money as an incentive.

Consider this example. Two old school chums meet after 20 years. One is in tatters, with a three-day growth of beard and a wine bottle peeking out from his coat pocket. The other is a thing of beauty from his styled hair to his freshly shined Gucci's. The obviously successful one speaks first, "What happened to you? You were the most brilliant student our school ever had." "Well," the other replied, "I went into space research and when the program ended I got dumped. But you, my friend, seem well off indeed, and, if you pardon my boldness, your performance in school was poor to say the least." "Well," the first man replied, "I just buy stuff for a dollar and sell it for two. On the 1 percent difference I make a living."

The Profit Motive

Nowhere does all of this come together more than in management's fairy tale of the profit motive. The problem is that that motive is often fulfilled by the most incompetent performance. When people in corporations perform incompetently, they inflate the cost of doing business. The corporation then raises its prices to cover these additional costs.

The profit system, as it operates, is not designed to encourage competence. It could be, but it isn't. There are many huge companies that annually mete out bonuses to all employees on the basis of their salary. The perceived relationship between that bonus and their performance is zero. Indeed, I heard one wage-and-salary expert "explain" that his firm's computerized formula allowed for only 5 percent excellent performance. Incredulous, I asked what would happen if there was 10 percent excellent performance. His answer was that half the employees would get the top bonus. But the president of one corporation said it best when asked how many people worked in his company. He said, "Oh, about half of them."

Here, then, is a picture of human performance that even a

child can understand. Unfortunately, we adults have the power and often screw it up royally. What we do, you see, is focus on behavior rather than results. Incentives are not really connected to accomplishments. When you pay me for how I *behave* rather than what I achieve, you make a jackass out of me. My one recourse is to get together with other donkeys and force you to pay more for my time. You then raise prices and we all slide down the spiral staircase of inflation.

Management

The single most common complaint within organizations is the inability to communicate effectively. Given the plethora of meetings, memos, and available media, one must wonder why such is the case. Managers on the whole tend to be fairly articulate people with reasonable language skills, yet messages seem to get garbled.

Here is a case in point. The president of a billion-dollar chemical company dictated the following memo to all employees at its corporate headquarters:

> Work begins at 9:00 A.M. and ends at 5:00 P.M. The allotted time for lunch is 30 minutes. If you can't keep to those hours I suggest you find work elsewhere.

Prior to its distribution, the president asked me to comment. My reply was that if people did not know the expected working hours, his letter would certainly clarify the matter. Further, I suspected much more was going on. His irate response was, "You're damn right!" Once calmed, he related how during a rare departure at 4:45 P.M. the previous week, he was nearly trampled by employees rushing to their cars. Not wishing to overreact (his words), he issued counters to the guards at the gate to keep track of latecomers, early leavers, and long lunchers. The number was sizable.

My advice to the president was to hold off firing his missile until we could determine what the problem was. A reasonable man, he agreed. Here is what we found:

1. Most latecomers worked in data processing. Since they often returned in the wee hours to get time on the computer, they did not feel compelled to be punctual every morning.
2. The street in front of the building had become a major feeder to the turnpike. Without a traffic light, entry onto that road after 5:00 P.M. was a nightmare (the president rarely left before 6:00).
3. With the completion of a company cafeteria, lunchtime was shortened from one hour. Many people had used that time to shop or go to the bank. The habit continued.

Needless to say, the letter was not sent. Instead, active efforts were made to accommodate the needs of the employees. Such is the nature of communication problems. For, in fact, they are not problems but symptoms, and most often they have little to do with the process of sending and receiving messages. Indeed, such dilemmas are just as likely to involve being too clear as not clear enough.

The symptom/cause dynamic is at the heart of organizational ineffectiveness. It is why bureaucrats deal in trivia, politicians speak without saying anything, and managers find their targets made of glass.

Ask most managers why an employee failed to perform and they will be quick to point out flaws in that individual's behavior. Since organizations expect logical behavior from machines, they extend the courtesy to people. But people don't behave logically (Rule 11). The result is much frustration. That's the bad news. The good news is it *doesn't matter*. It is performance, *not* behavior, that gets the job done. Further, eight out of ten times, it is the manager's performance—not the employee's—that caused the failure in the first place.

Consider this actual case. A team of behavioral scientists was studying nine sales districts in Great Britain. One district was consistently at the bottom in terms of sales performance. The researchers spent months traveling with salespeople and their managers. Having learned that presentations can be divided into features (what the product has) and benefits (what the product can do), they kept score. The results were astonishing. While top performers concentrated on presenting benefits, the poorer ones focused on features.

As an experiment, the research team shared their data with the managers of the bottom district. They suggested that these managers keep their own score when traveling with their sales force and encourage the salespeople to place greater emphasis on benefits.

The results surprised even the behavioral scientists. In less than a year, the experimental district became number one in sales! And this occurred without a single change in sales personnel.

This example points out two fundamental truths about improving performance. First, the worst-performing individual or group offers the most opportunity for improvement. That's simple arithmetic. If performance is 90 percent of standard, a 10-percent improvement will yield less than a 1-percent increase. However, if performance is 70 percent, the same improvement will result in a 7-percent increase.

Second, low skill level rarely causes poor performance. It was the *managers* that changed, not the salespeople. The salespeople already knew what the features and benefits were. They just couldn't see the connection to making the sale. That is the essence of Rule 17.

Rule 17: People rarely fail for technical reasons.

Organizations are quick to learn whether an individual can technically perform a job. In short order, people must prove they are competent to hammer a nail, drive a bus, or manage a plant. It is for nontechnical reasons that such behavior does not convert to acceptable performance. Such reasons most often fall into one of two categories: lack of incentive or lack of feedback. That is, people who are not performing up to standard either can't see a payoff for doing so (cold vs. warm calls) or can't see the impact of their effort (features vs. benefits). Quite simply then, improving productivity is the process of helping people see—not what you want them to see, but what is really there.

Conclusions

In his book *The Human Side of Enterprise* Douglas McGregor wrote, "Man will exercise self-direction and self-control in the service of objectives to which he is committed." He labels such behavior "Theory Y." McGregor reasons that the *assumptions* underlying such a statement are in direct contrast to the typical expectation that people will avoid work at all costs, a principle termed "Theory X."

The notions of self-direction and self-control give a lot of managers trouble. Because people bump into things, managers assume they are blind. Thus, they put great energy into pushing, prodding, and nudging employees. Paradoxically, they become resentful when these folks push back.

Part of the confusion surrounding this issue stems from the fact that it relates only to behavior, not to performance. McGregor assumed that behavior would be logical; it isn't (Rule 11). Psychologists have tried for over 50 years to prove that satisfied workers are more productive. Such proof has not been produced. In actual fact, the opposite is more likely: that is, unsatisfied workers may be more productive. Since people act to meet perceived needs (Rule 2), an unsatisfied worker is one who has needs that could be fulfilled at work. In this case, the business of improving performance would be served better by changing people's perceptions than by changing their behavior.

This is the real message of Theory Y. Give people clear, measurable objectives, an incentive for accomplishing them, and the tools to measure progress. Then get the hell out of their way.

References

Levinson, Harry, *The Great Jackass Fallacy*. Cambridge, Mass.: Harvard University Press, 1973.

McGregor, Douglas, *The Human Side of Enterprise*. New York: McGraw-Hill, 1960.

8
Conflict

You always hurt the one you love.

Famous sadist

Conflict is an ugly word. It conjures up images of taut faces and clenched fists. Indeed, it is so laden with negative implications that people get uptight just talking about it. Consider this recent case.

Three small companies were merged into a "miniconglomerate" to deal better with the competition. A corporate office was created. It included the president, the controller, an administrator, and three general managers (one for each of the businesses). The president had been one of the general managers and had named his number-two man as his successor before he ascended to the presidency. In one-on-one interviews I learned that the general managers were not thrilled with their loss of status and power, but they recognized that their survival depended on the merger.

An off-site "team-building" meeting was convened because the president was not satisfied that people were working together effectively. The session began with the president's presentation of a formal agenda, complete with overhead transparencies that outlined in detail what he wanted to cover. The agenda contained many more issues than could be reasonably discussed in the available time.

The meeting progressed at a rapid-fire rate. Each time disagreement arose, the topic was tabled for future discussion. Throughout the morning the general managers "sniped" at each other in half-jesting ways. At one point, a general manager's "beeper" sounded and he excused himself to call his office. As he reached the door, one of his peers remarked, "Sophisticated managers don't use those things anymore."

Just before noon, the president asked me to comment on the morning's activity. I told the meeting that I perceived much conflict that was not being dealt with. The group's overwhelming response was that I was greatly mistaken. With that, we adjourned for lunch.

Throughout the afternoon, managers would direct comments to me and point out that there was no conflict. Finally, with a deep sigh, one of them suggested that there was indeed conflict and that he for one was tired of not dealing with it. The others quickly joined in and agreed. And at that point, the group began to deal with process and moved toward building a team.

Tension

Conflict is a natural phenomenon that occurs when two or more forces act in opposite directions. The result is a state of tension. Individuals, groups, and organizations all experience it in one form or another. When the forces balance, there exists a condition of inactivity that significantly hampers performance. In the example above, each of the three general managers illustrated one such state. These are outlined in Figure 10.

Individuals act to meet perceived needs (Rule 2). But what happens when two such needs are mutually exclusive? Consider the general manager who was promoted because his boss became president. On the one hand, he wanted to exert his independence and run his own show. But if the merger did not "take," his old boss might very well return to his previous position. That required that he cooperate and be a team player. Torn between the two needs his behavior vacillated from arrogant to conciliatory. Such is the nature of *plus/plus conflict*, more popularly labeled Hobson's Choice.

A second manager faced a different dilemma. His business was the most vulnerable and a prime candidate for takeover. Although

Figure 10. States of conflict: (a) plus/plus; (b) minus/minus: (c) plus/minus.

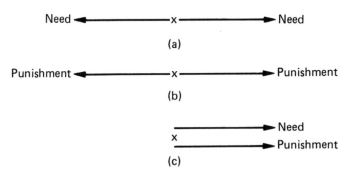

(a)

(b)

(c)

the merger prevented a takeover, the president was already expressing dissatisfaction with this manager's performance. The merger was the lesser of two evils but an evil none the less in the manager's eyes. This is the essence of *minus/minus conflict,* in which one punishment is suffered to avoid another.

The third general manager ran a business that suffered from a shrinking market. Faced with the choice of merging or closing down, his decision was easy. But there was a complicating factor. The new president located his office at the third manager's facility and took a very personal interest in its day-to-day operations, thus reducing the manager's freedom and independence. Such a trade-off is characteristic of *plus/minus conflict,* in which a need is met but a punishment must be suffered in the process.

Interpersonal Conflict

Although the principles of forces, tension, and the stress they produce are quite precise when they relate to machines, they do not extend to people. Three robots playing poker will perform in very predictable ways because the concept of coalition is not part of their repertoire. *Coalition* is defined as two or more parties joining forces. Indeed, such behavior requires a degree of creative effort, which is uniquely human. The good news is that such creativity can generate spectacular performance. The bad news is that it can cause such debilitation that performance will be exceedingly poor. The *capacity* for coalition is what lies at the heart of most interpersonal conflicts. It is the fear of being "ganged up" on. Also, such creative behavior and its lack of predictability can cause people to feel frustrated and stressful.

Games are sets of rules that determine how information can be used. When information is imperfect, uncertainty is created. Since people operate on perceptions rather than facts, such uncertainty is almost guaranteed. The various permutations of possible coalitions also increases the likelihood of uncertainty. In the final analysis, people act on hunches. Acting on a hunch is a gamble taken without a fully calculated risk. In general, people select one of three approaches to deal with all this uncertainty.

1. Random—leave it to fate.
2. Limits—estimate risk versus payoff.
3. Coalition—cooperate.

These are the choices when people find themselves in conflict with others and must make a decision. They can flip a coin (random), handicap the odds (limits), or strike a deal (coalition).

There is an apparent fourth choice: that is, to take no action. In reality, though, such a strategy is only a variation of the first. Choosing not to act leaves the result to chance.

Groups

The primary objective of any group is to maintain its orderly existence (Rule 4). Any threat to its survival is at the core of conflict within groups of people. In game parlance, conflict is defined as the existence of a zero-sum game. That is, in order for one party to win, another must lose. Such is the nature of poker, and it must be so. It is often the case in groups, but it need not be so.

A group's rules specify the conditions under which members can interact. Such rules were spelled out in Chapter 2 in terms of structure. That is, how a person may behave in a group is determined by role, authority, and status. When people deviate from the rules, they feel pressure from fellow members and a state of conflict exists.

In Chapter 2 it was also pointed out that a group defines its identity in terms of other groups. Perception of differences often leads to a "we-they" orientation. Distortions in this perception lead to exaggerating the positives of one's own group and minimizing the negatives. The opposite view is accorded other groups.

In organizations, groups regard each other as obstacles to attaining goals. They may even view each other as threats to their survival. Such are the seeds of power struggles.

Intergroup Conflict

People live and act on the basis of their perceptions. Since each of us perceives the world in a slightly different way, it is not always easy to agree on what reality is. Indeed, the *process* of agreement must occur through some external mechanism. For example, a newly sighted person has no idea what color is called green. However, once a particular hue is identified and labeled, this person has, in essence, *agreed* to call it "green."

When groups are in conflict, it is vital to understand how each perceives the situation—that is, what they see as reality. Three basic perceptions are possible:

1. Conflict is inevitable.
2. Conflict can be avoided.
3. Conflict can be resolved.

Democracy is a marvelous instrument of government that goes a long way toward protecting the freedom of individuals. It is based, however, on the premise that conflict is inevitable but agreement is not. The result is a continuing series of win-lose power struggles that are "resolved" by voting. Voting creates compromise and thus stifles the pursuit of excellence. Half a loaf is sometimes worse than none. Taking the middle road has done more to cause inflation and recession than any other single factor. Putting one foot in boiling water and the other on a block of ice does not average out to feeling quite comfortable.

A second perception is that while conflict is avoidable, there is no possibility of resolution when it does arise. The result is a stalemate in which one or both parties must withdraw. Such withdrawal can be physical (leaving) or psychological (indifference). Either way, there is a lessening of the interdependence between the groups. This is possible because no rule requires agreement. Such a rule *does* exist in the previous situation. Whether it compromises or not, Congress will reach a decision—eventually.

A third perception is that while conflict is inevitable, agreement is possible. In this case, groups are assumed to be highly dependent on each other and therefore cannot withdraw. The rules require resolution, and the result is most often a process of negotiation. This is the basis on which management and unions face each other.

How groups choose to perceive a state of conflict depends on the structure of the organization to which they belong. As mentioned previously, the behavior of group members will be determined by three factors:

1. role: job responsibilities
2. authority: power
3. status: position

These factors combine to create goals, norms, and values that are shared as part of group membership. Popularized as peer pressure, they powerfully influence the behavior of individuals and ultimately the performance of the group and the organization.

The Conflict Game

We now have all the elements with which to lay out the parameters of the conflict process in organizations. The next step is to determine the *level* of conflict:

Level	Game	Source of Tension
1. Individual	Solitaire	Rewards vs. Punishment
2. Interpersonal	Singles	Cooperation vs. Competition
3. Intragroup	Traitor	Cohesion vs. Independence
4. Intergroup	War	Integration vs. Differentiation

A hot topic in recent years has been the issue of stress management. A person under stress is experiencing individual conflict. In the absence of a clear-cut choice to avoid punishment or obtain a reward, he or she expends much energy to deal with the resulting high level of tension. The mere presence of such tension indicates that no resolution has been achieved and that the forces are in balance. In Biblical terms, this might be considered wrestling with God's angel. Psychoanalysts would refer to id, ego, and superego. Those with a preference for transactional analysis would focus on parent, adult, and child orientations.

Any way you slice it, people under stress are in conflict with themselves; it is a game of perceptual solitaire. But recent research into the use of biofeedback equipment is most remarkable. It shows that people who can *see* their level of tension through some visual or auditory monitoring device can learn to reduce it. Here, then, is a case of curing the symptom *and* the cause. It resembles the results of David McClelland's work (see Chapter 1), in which managers taught to act as if they were highly achievement-oriented would often achieve more than those who were not so taught. This is the nature of games played through perception, where symptom and cause are often indistinguishable. That is, rewards and punishments are simply value judgments in which one person's poison may be another's pleasure.

Interpersonal conflict is a game of one on one. Played as singles, individuals represent only themselves. That is, their loyalty is to their role rather than their group or organization.

Take this example. As an adjunct professor teaching a night course in organizational behavior, I represented pure profit. If sufficient students did not register, I was not employed. The college either made money or broke even on my efforts. Because of declining enrollment, the administration had enacted a 10-percent salary cut for full-time instructors. In a staff meeting, I suggested a marketing campaign to sell local companies on using the night school to train new managers. The immediate response was that there was no money in the budget for such a program. I then offered to match them dollar for dollar to actively recruit additional enrollees. The staff unanimously responded that such action was not its responsibility. In the restaurant business, this is known as "this ain't my table."

Interpersonal conflict is relatively easy to resolve. Choices tend to be clear-cut: compete or cooperate. In tennis, cooperation is intolerable, if not illegal. Players stand at opposite ends of the court and hammer away at each other. In restaurants, smart managers pool tips to create a common goal and encourage cooperation. Indeed, the absence or presence of a common goal determines whether individuals will push for agreement or fight to the death.

Intragroup conflict adds a new dimension to the game. Here individuals represent a group rather than just themselves. Should they violate the norms they will be perceived as traitors. The orderly existence of groups demands loyalty before anything else. Indeed, people are often described in terms of the groups to which they belong. If you need further proof, try calling someone in a large organization whom you do not know well. The first query out of his or her secretary's mouth will be, "Who are you with?"

In the merger example presented earlier in this chapter, the general managers deeply felt the growing conflict between their needs for independence and the cohesive demands of their role in corporate management. The beeper incident represents more than two men with strong egos playing a hard game of singles. (In that sense, such behavior is indeed childish.) As organizational representatives, they were also deeply involved in intragroup conflict. Later it was learned that they often competed in the same markets. Such is the nature of groups in isolation. When there is no clear enemy, they often fight among themselves.

The most visible level of conflict is between groups. As was mentioned earlier, groups often develop their identity in terms of how they are differentiated from other groups. This process creates very clear enemies and often leads to war.

Organizations were described in Chapter 3 as existing in a force field balanced between the needs for specialization of labor and unity of command. The tension that exists between forces of integration and differentiation is at the core of intergroup conflict in organizations. But it is not always the prime cause. The we-they phenomenon is often a natural result of group formation. This process is called polarization. It requires very little other than some feature that distinguishes one group from another. Consider the following true story.

Although my efforts to rally my fellow teachers toward a marketing campaign were not successful, I forged ahead on my own anyway. The result was too good. Registrations for my class reached twice the capacity of available classrooms. An additional instructor was assigned to teach a second section. Our dilemma was how to split the groups. Always the optimist, I suggested we use this dilemma to teach the students something about group behavior. Rather than resolving the matter for them, we assigned the students the task of dividing into two classes.

A logical way for them to proceed would have been to put the ball back in our court by requiring us to "sell" them on our virtues as teachers and educators. However, that would have created a win-lose situation focusing on which students would get the "better" teacher. A random strategy such as who was closest to the door would have quickly solved the dilemma, but it would have been an open admission of failure to solve the problem in a cognitive way. With time running out, one young man stood up and announced that he was tired of "playing games" and was going next door to await half the group and an instructor. With great relief, others soon followed.

Notice the similarity between the young man and the general manager who announced that there was conflict in the merger group. Once people recognize that all their energy is being directed toward creating a state of inactivity, movement in one direction or the other is not far behind. This is the secret of conflict resolution.

In the story of my night class, the real learning came a few weeks later—not for the students but the teachers. Having obtained a marvelous film on organizational development, I offered to show it to both classes. Since the other instructor's room was larger, the movie was shown there. Afterward my section returned to our own classroom to discuss the film. The silence was deafening. Something was wrong. "What's going on?" I asked. Suddenly the floodgates burst open. Why did we have to go to "their" room? "They" were terrible hosts. It was "our" film, and "we" should have gotten the best seats. On and on flowed the anger and resentment toward "them." In but a few short hours of class time we had created enemies. A bunch of strangers had polarized into two groups whose identity stemmed from the embarrassment of being unable to separate themselves on a rational basis.

Since groups polarize as a natural part of their formation, differences between them become grossly exaggerated. Corporate versus division, line versus staff, office versus factory, and upstairs versus downstairs are all "logical" differences that are used to explain what is a psychological process. They are the words, not the music, of organizational conflict.

Organizational Conflict

A bullfrog sat along the banks of a raging stream and pondered his dilemma. He wished to cross to the other side and could swim quite well, but he would not be able to see above the frothing white water. The risk of crashing into a rock and drowning was very great.

Along came a scorpion who also wanted to cross the stream. He could not swim. The frog and the scorpion discussed the matter and decided to join forces. The scorpion, perched atop the frog, could see clearly and navigate between the treacherous rocks.

Halfway across the stream, the scorpion stung the frog. As they sank to their deaths, the frog wailed, "Why?" The scorpion responded matter-of-factly, "Because it is my nature."

The second step in understanding organizational conflict is to identify what is perceived as the nature of things. That is, what level of trust exists? The degree of trust will determine what strategy is taken to resolve the conflict. As with individuals, organizational approaches tend to involve random choice, setting limits, or forming coalitions.

The Win-Lose Game

The most common approach to settling intergroup conflict is to perceive the situation in terms of a win-lose orientation. As mentioned previously, this occurs when people see their dilemma as a zero-sum game. Under such conditions, groups will let fate decide the outcome (random), negotiate a settlement (coalition), or bring in an arbitrator (limits). A most striking example of this process is the struggle between unions and management. The fable of the frog and the scorpion is not all fantasy. The survival of organizations is often threatened by two groups that need each other yet find it difficult to detach themselves from the win-lose game.

Midwest Molybdenum, a division of a large conglomerate, found itself the odd man out in its struggle with two competitors to maintain market share (Rule 14). In spite of several technological advantages, Midwest spent substantially more than the competition to produce the metal. The cause was clearly attributable to very high labor costs. Discussions with the Amalgamated Alloy Workers brought no relief. In desperation the conglomerate sold the division and took a $100 million loss. Shortly thereafter, the purchaser moved the plant and put all of the hourly employees out of work.

Three years ago, the teachers in the Burnt Umber School District threatened to strike unless they received a substantial pay increase. The school board, with great humility, convinced them that the money was just not available. The teachers settled for an amount that was less than the rate of inflation. At the end of the first year under the new contract, the school district had a surplus of $5 million. Twenty-four hours after the contract expired the teachers were forming a picket line. When the school board pleaded poverty again, the teachers suggested that it place its offer where the sun doesn't shine.

The essential goal of conflict resolution is movement. To achieve it, forces need to be unbalanced. The problem with an organizational win-lose game is that positions are fixed, which creates low levels of trust and prohibits agreement. The process becomes one of emphasizing differences and ignoring commonalities. People become blinded to options other than trying to win and avoid losing. Players are faced with a plus/minus dilemma, but they alter their perception of risk versus payoff to gain movement rather than to make any fundamental changes in the situation. They would rather die than depend on the enemy for help.

Setting Limits—Arbitration

When the value of conflict resolution begins to approach the risk of losing or the cost of winning, groups may decide to go to a third party to render judgment. In such cases, they see any decision as better than none.

Although arbitration is often regarded as a very efficient strategy, it is really a destructive process. In many cases, it is just a continuation of a win-lose game. Groups' perceptions are so distorted they they are liable to envision that the third party "must" see it their way. Another possible outcome is that both sides lose, but they lose less than they would if they had battled it out themselves.

Managers with more than one subordinate often find themselves in the position of judge and jury when peer groups cannot resolve their differences. If such managers allow themselves to be seduced into donning a robe and grabbing a gavel, they will merely force the conflict underground. If they determine a winner, there will be a loser. If they determine no winner, there will be two losers. The only guarantee is that in the long run the manager will lose—a prime attribute of a minus/minus game.

Fate

One of the negative payoffs for managers who choose arbitration is that they may serve as a lightning rod for all of the hostility generated by the warring groups, both the losers and the winners, who may feel their victory is hollow because they didn't do it themselves. Ironically this situation may actually cause both groups to resolve their differences on their own and combine their energy to defeat the common enemy, the boss. This often occurs in organizations that constantly replace managers of a group that itself remains relatively intact.

A way to avoid this risk is to resolve stalemates by resorting to random choice and letting fate decide. In games of chance, this is a very real part of the rules. In organizations, the more common variation is to make no decision and let the chips fall where they may. Such a process both allows conflicting groups to save face if they lose and protects the manager from mutiny. This is how organizations end up not knowing what business they are in and ultimately failing to survive (Rule 10). Rather than hurt anyone's feelings, resources are dribbled away and conflicts are brushed under the carpet.

Coalition

Most cooperative strategies for resolving conflict deal with perceptual change. They assume that agreement is possible and become a self-fulfilling prophecy. Within this context, there are three courses of action that groups may take: détente, compromise, and problem solving.

Détente is a fancy word for peaceful coexistence. It is a strategy of withdrawal by avoiding conflict rather than one of resolution. Perceptual change is accomplished by minimizing or ignoring differences and emphasizing commonalities. It is a dangerous game that stifles creativity and causes "dry rot" from within. Bubbling beneath the surface are all the powerful feelings of anger and resentment that threaten to erupt at any moment. A state of détente will last only as long as neither group has sufficient power to win or both continue to view losing as too great a risk.

A second strategy that groups of equivalent power adopt is compromise. In essence, compromise is a collaborative approach to playing a game of limits. A prime example of this tactic in organizations is the "hiring freeze."

During times of economic downturn, many large organizations prohibit managers from hiring new people. The unspoken message is that were this freeze not in effect, managers would make hiring decisions that were not in the best economic interests of the company. Carry this logic further and you have managers who are allowed to make such poor judgments during good times. In essence, compromise is a lose-lose game. In order to achieve harmony and reduce the perception of conflict, performance is allowed to diminish—often at a time when the organization can least afford it.

As mentioned previously, when a manager serves as arbitrator between two peer groups in conflict, they may form a coalition against him or her; polarity disappears as if by magic. History is replete with examples of "natural" enemies joining forces to fend off a common enemy. Unfortunately, once the threat is gone the conflict returns. The key element in this process is that of commonality. In this case, it is a negative commonality of mutual threat. But it is also possible for groups to form a coalition around a positive commonality such as a mutual need or common goal. This strategy is called problem solving.

The process of problem solving requires a significant perceptual change to disengage parties from their polarized views. Notice that in all other cases, the major focus is on solutions rather than the problem; the objective is to reduce conflict, not to remove the underlying cause. The alternative is summarized in Rule 18.

√ *Rule 18:* The secret to problem solving is defining the
problem, not the solution.

The presence of a common goal is one essential requisite that groups
need to perceive that an agreement is possible. The other is the
realization that they are indeed in a state of conflict. In this context,
problems become barriers to achieving the common goal. However,
removing these obstacles is easier said than done because we are
dealing with perceptions rather than some objective reality. Thus,
problem solving must begin with perceptual change.

Perceptual Change

When individuals are engaged in interpersonal conflict, they do not
see themselves or each other clearly. A most effective technique for
improving their perception is to require that they argue each other's
point. The process is called role reversal, and it enables people to
see how others see them and to experience the others' point of view.
Often it will allow them to identify common goals and to begin the
process of defining problems.

Reversal is also an effective tool for helping to resolve organizational conflict, but here the issues are more complex. Not only
structural issues of role, authority, and status must be dealt with,
but goals, norms, and identity must be considered as well. The
following incident is an example of such an approach.

Ignition Industries built a new electronics plant in Colorado
and was greatly concerned by excessive downtime on the machines
that produced parts. This problem was especially critical because
government contracts explicitly forbid overruns. Thus, any amount
of product not shipped on time was lost forever and would not be
accepted later.

It quickly became apparent that a major issue affecting downtime was the tremendous conflict between maintenance and production. Each side felt the other was at fault.

Our strategy was to get each group to clarify in writing how it perceived itself and how it saw the other group. The next step was to bring the groups together to discuss their perceptions. The intensity of feelings was so great that a number of managers predicted that the two groups might come to physical blows. With some trepidation, we proceeded anyway.

The result was nothing less than astounding. Within 24 hours of the first confrontation, the two groups were actively engaged in problem solving. Here are the before and after positions:

BEFORE CONFRONTATION

Maintenance:

Sees self as "martyr"—not given time to fix machines properly the first time.
Sees production as indifferent to this dilemma.

Production:

Sees self as "scapegoat"—forced to operate unreliable equipment.
Sees maintenance as indifferent to this dilemma.

AFTER CONFRONTATION

Maintenance:

Sees the problem as untested equipment. Goal is to meet production schedule.

Production:

Sees the problem as untested equipment. Goal is to meet production schedule.

Prior to putting the two groups in the same room, each had an opportunity to review the perceptions listed by the other group. Production was amazed that maintenance felt the primary objective of the plant was "to get the stuff out the door." Maintenance was equally amazed that production was sympathetic to its concerns.

Working jointly, they were quick to agree that their mutual survival depended on timely shipments. Once they established this common goal, they were able to identify the major barrier as a manufacturing process that had never been tested outside the research laboratory. Thus, maintenance was expected to "debug" the system while production operated to a theoretical standard. Working together, the two departments identified the parts of the process that did not function properly. Specific chunks of time were set aside to fix them. Within six months the plant was operating on schedule for the first time in its history.

Conclusions

Intergroup conflict is a major drain on the time, talent, and energy of an organization. It can develop almost overnight as a natural part of group formation and polarization. Effective conflict resolution can take place just as swiftly if there is some mechanism for unlocking the combatants so that they have an opportunity to test their perceptions against reality. Reversal is one such mechanism. It requires high levels of trust, openness, and willingness to take risks. For those who try, the rewards can be substantial. Problem solving is the only "win-win" strategy in the game.

9

Structure

A house is not a home.   Famous madam

The structure of an organization is meant to reflect the work that is done—in other words, the content. It will also have a significant impact on process, particularly for information flow (communications) and decision making. The *shape* of the structure will determine responsibility (roles), authority (power), and status.

The traditional concept of hierarchy is based on a military design. Indeed, this structure is documented in the Bible: Moses faced the task of directing and controlling thousands of soldiers, and he was counseled to put someone in charge of 1,000 who in turn should put someone in charge of 100 who in turn should put someone in charge of 10. And it ought not go unnoticed that managers in industrial organizations often use military jargon. They speak of "battles," "troops," and "the guys in the trenches."

Hierarchy works well in the military because the formal structure clearly reflects process as well as content. Roles, power, and status are worn on the sleeves and shoulders of its members. The rules are spelled out in detail and those who do not go by the book are swiftly punished. Consider the following case.

In trying to decide on officer promotions, the army found that performance appraisal data were not very useful. Captains were always rated higher than lieutenants, majors were always rated higher than captains, and so on. The personnel research operation was asked to devise a better way, and it developed a "forced-choice" rating scale that masked from the rater just how high or low his evaluation was. That is, pairs of statements were listed reflecting job performance, but it was not obvious which were positive and which negative.

The result was an overall rating that did not correlate with rank alone. Unfortunately it caused raters so much discomfort that the approach was abandoned. The cultural norms of power and rank were too strong to change. Ironically a number of industrial organizations picked up on the technique and used it as part of their appraisal process.

Hierarchical structure is useful because it meets the organization's needs for unity of command while keeping span of control within manageable limits. It assumes a relative uniformity of tasks. Jobs in the military are more often defined by what rank is required rather than by specific skills and abilities. In more complex organizations with a wide variety of tasks, however, hierarchy will be less effective.

Structure and Process

Organizations are groups that can survive the loss of one member (Rule 5). Structure facilitates survival. It provides the continuity that enables a person to come off the bench and assume the responsibility for a function. Baseball teams and battalions have such clarity of roles that these transitions can occur relatively smoothly. Both types of organizations have formal structures that are highly congruent with actual process. That is, what you see is what you get. This is true in spite of the fact that baseball teams and battalions differ greatly in shape.

But what of organizations whose formal structure does not fit reality? Classical organization theory matches structure with tasks, not people. The basic building block is the supervisor-subordinate pair. It creates an environment that supports values of passivity, subservience, and dependency. Such a culture meets the needs of children better than those of adults. So much has been written about paternalistic management that one forgets that it takes a house full of kids to make it work.

The irony of our history of labor-management strife is that when the work force matured, the only role model it had was management's. Thus, it was destined to repay injustice with injustice. Without the capability for problem solving, the child is doomed to repeat the sins of the parent.

As discussed in Chapter 8, the flames of conflict are fueled by uncertainty, or not knowing the odds. The heat is intensified by dry, brittle structure. It thwarts people's ability to anticipate, flex, and adapt. The net result is that performance declines as uncertainty increases. The bottom line is that formal hierarchical structure is effective for routine, repetitive, predictable tasks. But under conditions of accelerating change and task complexity, it begins to fall apart. The cracks appear in the two weakest links: communication and decision making.

Communication

Ask managers in a hierarchical organization to identify their most significant problem and they are almost sure to say poor communications. Indeed, the primary complaint to top management is that they don't know what is going on "down there." Why is this so? There is a plethora of organizational mechanisms for such process; meetings, memos, and media abound.

First, consider the essential communication process itself (see Figure 11). A message is sent and a message is received. Rarely is it the same message. Words carry so many different meanings that misunderstanding is almost guaranteed. To counter misunderstanding, there must be an additional element—feedback. One or both parties need to validate that there is equivalent meaning on both sides. Quite simply, poor interpersonal communication exists because there is no feedback. Feedback, not communication, is the problem.

Feedback problems become magnified a hundredfold in the

Figure 11. **The communication process.**

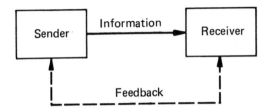

traditional hierarchical organization. We see in Figure 12 how people must contend with communication not only as individuals but also as group members. Level and position become very important factors. Essentially there are four variations: boss-subordinate, peer, diagonal, and horizontal. Each is greatly influenced by role, authority, and status.

The authority of a boss over a subordinate often reduces opportunities for feedback. Communication tends to be one-way. Confused messages are attributed to the listening ability of the subordinate rather than to the clarity of the boss. Effective communication requires that the three issues of structure—role, authority, and status—be dealt with. One problem, for example, is that bad news

Figure 12. **Communication in a hierarchy.**

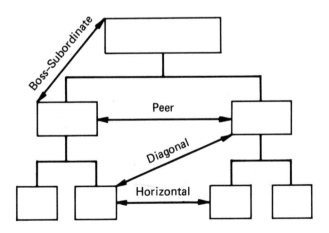

is valued over no news. By suppressing negative information, managers who get surprises more often than not have asked for them.

Communication between peers is most often distorted by the conflict that exists between them. Indeed, openness and trust are foolish in a zero-sum game.

Diagonal communication involves messages between different levels without a direct chain-of-command relationship. As a hybrid between boss-subordinate and peer communications, it often combines the worst features of each.

Horizontal communication occurs between peers who do not share a common immediate boss. At the lowest levels of the organization, these messages are often quite clear. With no apparent authority or power, individuals enjoy sharing the "straight poop." This is the root of the grapevine of information that top management wants but rarely gets.

Information Flow

The dilemma of hierarchy is that as uncertainty increases so does the amount of information needed to reduce it. Four strategies are employed to cope with this problem.

1. information reduction
2. decentralization
3. mechanization
4. short-circuiting

The simplest way to deal with information overload is to restrict information flow. This policy is often accomplished by rules and regulations and lies at the heart of most bureaucracies. Decisions are made by the book and thus require only minimum data. Exceptions are not tolerated because they create the need for more information. A more productive variation of this strategy is delegation. By moving decision making to lower rungs of an organization, higher levels need less information.

A second approach is to segment the organization through decentralization; division into product groups is a prime example. This strategy shifts the focus from input (specific functions such as production, engineering, and so on) to output (the product). Opportunities for conflict are reduced, as is the division of labor. Both result in the need for less information.

A third strategy is to mechanize information flow. Managers who once lamented being kept in the dark can now wallow in data thanks to computers. Of course, without feedback mechanisms there are plenty of opportunities to overload, which beclouds rather than illuminates the relevant communications.

Finally, there are a whole host of structural games that I call short-circuiting. These include junkets, liaisons, task forces, temporary teams, integrations, linking pins, and matrices. All are designed to change the role, status, and authority of managers while working within a hierarchical structure. The game is called "beating the system"; optimists call it "changing the system." Like putting a penny in a fuse box, it works—but not without risk. Let's explore these games in more depth.

One thing a manager can do to combat lack of useful data is to go out and get it for himself or herself. By making direct contact with lower levels of the organization, a manager can find out what is going on, or at least try to. These junkets can be formal affairs, such as the plant tour, or surprise visits. In either case, their utility is very much a function of the manager's ability to diagnose with little or no data. The risk is the effects of these trips on the authority of all the managers at intervening levels.

An alternate course is to create a specialized role of liaison officer to facilitate communication among functions. This position requires a unique skill that does not occur frequently in nature. One must be a conduit without getting electrocuted in the process.

Task forces are a way to formalize horizontal communication. At the lower levels, they make good use of the natural clarity of messages at the bottom and can be a powerful approach to problem solving. At higher levels, they just intensify sibling rivalry.

In Chapter 3 it was pointed out that a team can be a thing of beauty or a source of much frustration. Given a common goal and regular problem solving, the trust and openness that develop can significantly support accurate communication. But when a team is only temporary, the likelihood of such process is reduced.

A refinement of the temporary-team approach is to create an integrating role, which gives someone the power to pull the group together; the source of this power is often technical expertise. Such a role sharpens the common goal by centralizing the need for integration in one person. In a sense, it is a return to the simpler days of entrepreneurship, where the founder's genius made it all happen.

Unfortunately, as uncertainty increases it becomes more difficult to exercise expert power. The role requires formal authority to coordinate joint decisions. Such a role has been labeled "linking pin." It differs from the integrating role in that power is formalized. For example, the manager is given his own budget to "buy" expertise from other groups.

Lastly, there is the approach of creating a dual-authority relationship called a matrix organization. It is designed to balance the power between hierarchical specialization and linking-pin integration. Individuals may have *two* bosses, one for function (engineering manager, for example) and one for task (plant manager, for example). When an individual or group reports to both project and technology areas, there are a number of process consequences. First, there are split loyalties that may increase conflict. Second, while the volume of information flow may be reduced, the *quality* required is much higher. That is, effective communication in matrix organizations is supercritical in such areas as work assignments, priorities, and performance appraisal.

Decision Making

The trade-off for poor communications under a hierarchical structure is sharply focused decision making. At least on paper, the person at the top is responsible for all decisions. A decision can be delegated, but the *responsibility* for the result cannot. This is the true power of hierarchy. In crisis situations, there is rarely time to be participative; participation is a tremendously time-consuming process.

Decision making is perhaps the least understood of all the management processes. The fundamental issue is confusion between hierarchy and autocracy. The former describes structure while the latter describes management style.

Groups do not *make* decisions, but they can participate in the process. This type of participation is not the managerial con game in which a subordinate is asked for an opinion after the boss's mind is already made up. Rather, it is involvement in the process that leads up to the decision.

In participative management, a boss may say the following to his or her subordinates, "I am strongly drawn to option A for the following reasons. . . . If any of you disagree, it is your responsibility to convince me otherwise. Should I still opt for A, it is because you failed to dissuade me. That does not relieve you of your commitment to make it work."

Decision making is almost always a one-person task. A participative approach is valuable because it not only uses the sharp focus of hierarchical structure but also builds feedback loops to facilitate communication; this is why management theorists love the approach. Unfortunately, theory and practice do not often match. Here is a case in point.

The Toonerville Trolley Works was about to go broke. As the major contractor for building rapid-transit cars for a new subway system, its survival was threatened by cost overruns. The president of the Transportation Group vented his anger on his subordinate, the vice-president of the Trolley Division, who in turn had harsh words with the plant manager in Toonerville. The result was that the trolley works got a new plant manager, but the real culprit was the president, who priced the job in the first place. Contrary to the *theory* of hierarchy, actual practice often leads to action taken from the bottom up rather than the other way around. When top management does not take responsibility for its decisions, the game becomes crooked. It happens enough to warrant a rule of its own.

> *Rule 19:* Managers who live or die by the decisions of
> others are in a crooked game.

This process is called *accountability*. When people put their chips on the table, they have every right to decide how the cards will be played. When the boss deals from a stacked deck, subordinates would do well to have great faith or lots of chips.

Structure and Content

Although organizations are built to perform tasks, the *type* of task can significantly affect the relationship between structure and performance. Tasks are a function of focus—that is, the values and norms of the organization. Most tasks fall into at least one of four categories: creativity, craftsmanship, continuity, and customer service. Consider again the business of making cars.

A major barrier to innovative automotive design is the huge, complex hierarchy that envelops the folks who have the millions to turn dream into reality. If there is ever going to be a car that is powered by something other than an internal combustion engine, it will be born in the back of somebody's bicycle shop—as was its predecessor.

A recent newspaper article presented a front-page account of interviews with the chief executive officers of several large corporations. They were dissatisfied with their marketing functions, which, they felt, did not develop new products. More specifically they bemoaned the lack of risk taking, creativity, and "entrepreneurial spirit."

Paradoxically, each of these corporate giants once had individuals with these characteristics: they are the ones who left to start their own companies. Many of them have been very successful. The issue is not that they don't exist, but that hierarchical structure has difficulty with such independent and creative behavior. As students of Rule 19, the innovators either refused to play in a crooked game or were tapped out.

Cars and craftsmanship do not often go hand in hand; the average new automobile has more than a dozen defects. But high quality is possible, as proved by the existence of such handmade jewels as the Rolls-Royce. The key to such quality is not just the people who have applied specialized skills for decades, but the process that fits so neatly into hierarchical structure. Management gets clear lines of decision making because important details are left to the person doing the job. Indeed, the fit was so perfect that the British government took over Rolls when the company was about to declare bankruptcy. It was a marriage made in heaven—a quality product that can't turn a profit and a bureaucracy that doesn't know how to.

The focus of automobile production is continuity, not quality. When cars are mass produced, careful planning is required. Once successful, work remains unchanged. Individual jobs are routine and repetitive. Decisions tend to be made at the top with little delegation of authority. Rules, regulations, and detailed procedures are the order of the day. Both hierarchy and autocracy describe the process.

It was pointed out in Chapter 6 that an automobile dealership is a different business from production. A dealership is an example of the fourth possible focus—customer service. Dealers must keep an ear to the marketplace and be constantly aware of customer needs. Creativity is greatly valued and turnover a continuing threat. Opting for a hierarchical structure is a strategy most often doomed to failure in such organizations.

Design

It is very tempting to treat organizational design as if one were seated at a drafting table with a blank sheet of paper. While such an exercise can be great fun, its utility is questionable. People and organizations do not exist in a vacuum; they are products of their history, culture, and personality. The challenge for management is to *redesign* and modify organizations in order to adapt to a changing environment. But first they *must* know what game they are in. Too many organizations fool around with structure and do more harm than good. Consider Rule 20.

Rule 20: When in doubt, leave it alone.

Changing the structure of an organization is a slow and painful process. A favorite slogan of managers is that people resist change. This is not necessarily true. They resist change when the risk is relatively great but the payoff obscure. The systems, strategies, and gimmicks offered by theorists promise great improvement of productivity, but they offer little proof of performance. They aren't supposed to. They are *concepts* not cookbooks, rationales not recipes. Linking pins and matrices are brilliantly conceived plans, but they do involve risk. Before short-circuiting the system, a wise management should make sure the wiring can take the load.

Management and Structure

The only fallacy in the drafting-table approach to organization design is that the wrong person holds the pencil. The primary task is to describe what is, not what should be. It requires the practitioner, not the theorist, to do the drawing. The task can be simplified by using the following format. One need only connect the dots to complete the picture. Our goal is diagnosis, not artistry.

ORGANIZATIONAL DIAGNOSIS

Planning

1. What business are you in?
2. What is the focus (creativity, craftsmanship, continuity, or customer service)?

3. Where is it on its life cycle (shooting craps, pumping iron, clipping coupons, or milking cows)?
4. What is its past performance?

Organizing

1. How is it structured (role, authority, and status)?
2. What shape does it have (hierarchical, team, committee, matrix, and so on)?
3. What is the culture (goals, norms, values)?

Directing

1. Describe the communication process (open vs. closed).
2. Where are decisions made (top vs. bottom)?

Controlling

1. How is feedback handled (none, boss to subordinate, self-generated)?

One of my favorite diagnostic questions to ask a client is, "What is your organization's primary goal?" A common response from middle managers is, "To satisfy the customer." When I suggest that cutting prices would achieve that, the answer quickly changes to, "To make a profit." As a psychologist, I have been trained to attach significance to a person's first response. And indeed there is much meaning in such loosely held beliefs as customer satisfaction. Such beliefs are symptomatic of managers, particularly middle managers, who are quick to adopt sophisticated techniques and slogans while not fully understanding the basic rudiments of the game they are playing. Putting the cart before the horse is a sure way to get your behind bitten.

Middle Managers

The structure of an organization has its most significant impact on middle-level managers. For them, role, authority, and status are least clear. Top management knows it has the power, and those at the bottom are quick to discover they have little or none. To balance things out, those at the lowest level have valid data about what is really going on, while those at the top can only guess. In between, middle managers run themselves ragged trying to shift the balance. In the next section we will deal with the process of change and how managers can save their breath.

PART IV

CHANGE

The more things change, the more they stay the same.

Famous dress designer

10

Individual Change

There's gonna be some changes made. Famous toll collector

Let's review the bidding, as it were, with respect to human behavior.

Rule 1: People always act in their own best interest, given the facts as they know them.
Rule 2: People act to meet perceived needs.
Rule 3: People meet needs by getting rewards and avoiding punishment.
Rule 11: People do not behave logically; they behave psychologically.

Traditional psychotherapy has tried for over a century to cause people to change their behavior. The recorded results have been meager, to say the least. Managers have not had a much better track record in "motivating" employees to behave differently. Fortunately for both, it really doesn't matter. People don't enter therapy to change, but rather to cope better. And managers really don't want enthusiasm, they want results. It is very logical to assume that greater job satisfaction will increase productivity, but it just ain't so. Indeed, one can make a valid argument that "grumpy" workers achieve better results—particularly if they are grumpy about their current performance.

People, groups, and organizations exist in a state of equilibrium. Forces for change are balanced by forces for keeping the status quo. To create change, then, is to fiddle with the forces, not the people.

Place a glass barrier between a chicken and a bowl of food and it will beat its brains out trying to go through the glass. Do the same with a dog and it will simply walk around the barrier and chow down. It is just not in the chicken's repertoire to go around barriers it can see through.

The manager of a carpentry shop once pointed out a young man who had been trying to cut through a board with a handsaw but with little success. Closer inspection revealed that he was using the wrong edge; the teeth were pointing up. The manager's only comment was that this was further evidence that the youth would never learn to work with wood. Fortunately a passer-by suggested the lad try turning the saw over. It may go down as the shortest job-training course in history.

Change is nothing more than movement from one state of equilibrium to another. It occurs at two distinct levels. First, there is intrasystem change, or change that occurs within an individual's range of options (such as the dog walking around the barrier). Second, there is extrasystem change, which involves changing the system itself. To prevent the chicken from starving, one must physically remove the glass.

In the case of the carpenter's apprentice, the manager tried to get others to accept the premise that change could not occur within the system. He was quickly proved wrong. Of course, there is much more to the story. The manager's motivation was not to teach carpentry but rather to undermine the apprentice program. Further, one must question the young man's lack of achievement motivation given that he persevered at an apparently impossible task. The point, however, is that a frequent, major barrier to change is action taken at the wrong level. While a very simple intrasystem intervention got the board cut, no amount of training or conditioning will teach a chicken to circumvent transparent barriers.

In the game of management, one must be able to distinguish

between playing by the rules (intrasystem) and breaking them (extrasystem). Since the targets are made of glass, one has to be very clear about when to hit them, when to go around them, and when to have them removed. This lies at the very heart of effective problem solving. Here is another example.

East Coast Industries was run by a man who had a deep and abiding commitment to providing job opportunities for members of minorities who had migrated from the South. The problem was that, as a group, they were excessively late to work. It was proposed that a training program be developed to "teach" these people the importance of punctuality.

The president decided to delay this program and short-circuited the system by speaking directly to the people involved. He soon learned two very significant facts. First, the latecomers did not own alarm clocks. Second, most of them had been raised in rural areas, and they were accustomed to rising with the sun. Unfortunately, the morning light had great difficulty shining into the windows of closely spaced urban apartment buildings. Having learned this information, the president instructed his associates to purchase and distribute alarm clocks. The cost was a fraction of the proposed training. Almost immediately, tardiness declined significantly.

The president went outside the system. Those closest to the problem could visualize change only within the walls of the factory. They made the usual and false assumption that people who do not play by the rules do so because they don't understand them. They failed to grasp Rule 21.

> *Rule 21:* System change must be introduced from the outside and will appear illogical and unpredictable to those within it.

Being part of a system means being a member of a group. In order to survive, groups create rules that encourage predictability. The same is true of organizations. The problem is that there are rules that prohibit the changing of rules. Without a change of rules, there can be no change in the system. It is a vicious cycle that stifles creativity in order to achieve equilibrium.

Problems and Dilemmas

The secret to problem solving is to define the problem, not the solution (Rule 18). Indeed, problems can develop solely as a result of inappropriate attempts to change an already present dilemma. To understand this, one must distinguish between a problem and a dilemma. A dilemma refers to a condition of conflict that may be intrapersonal, interpersonal, intergroup, or organizational. It is a state of discomfort in which the pain is often not great enough to spur immediate action. A problem is a *stalemate* that is created and maintained because a dilemma does not get resolved. That is, the dilemma remains and often gets worse in spite of a barrage of solutions being thrown at it. Thus, a dilemma becomes a problem by virtue of the continued investment of time and energy toward an unsuccessful resolution. A crooked game is not a problem to those who do not try to win (the corollary of Rule 19). It is the notion of dilemma that is the basis for the advice in Rule 20 (When in doubt, leave it alone).

There are essentially four ways to create a problem out of a dilemma. First, a person may deny that the dilemma exists. In this case, the problem arises out of all the energy expended to avoid the pain. Psychologists call this phenomenon *repression*, in which people behave in ways exactly opposite to their true feelings. The net result is an *increase* in tension that can eventually explode into open conflict.

Second, one may try to resolve a dilemma that cannot be changed or does not exist. Eric Berne calls this a game of *blemish*, in which a person devotes great energy toward a real or imagined dilemma that never goes away.

A third source of problem formation occurs when one attempts to solve an extrasystem dilemma from within. Poor performance on the job becomes a problem *after* pep talks and motivational gimmicks fail.

Finally, an intrasystem dilemma may become a problem when solutions are implemented from the outside. Thus, we try to change attitudes or raise morale with no consequent improvement in performance. Indeed, performance may actually improve, but the problem remains because it occurs for the "wrong" reasons.

Myths: Whistling in the Dark

Denial is a defense mechanism and, as such, it is inherently neither bad nor good. Part of the process of socialization is the teaching of rules about what can and can't be talked about. This training creates norms and values that sometimes lead to myths. A myth is a denial of reality in order to preserve logic and predictability. Thus, fairy tales always have happy endings and justice is always served. A myth becomes a problem only when people believe it and act or don't act on that basis. "Happy workers are more productive workers" is just such a myth.

In Chapter 9 it was pointed out that poor communication is really a problem of feedback. One might naturally assume, then, that more feedback is better. But, in fact, the real culprit is not so much lack of clarity as mixed messages: not only may people not understand us, but also they may but we don't know it. Thus, the angry president who was about to send out his "shape up or ship out" letter regarding employees' work hours clearly communicated his anger. But he hid behind the logic of work times as a way to deny his feelings regarding being trampled in the hallway.

Management is replete with myths about what is acceptable behavior. Safety is a good example. In the press room of a large printing establishment, there was a huge sign that read "Safety First." Among the guidelines on the sign was the admonition to never put one's hands into a moving press. However, press operators frequently reached into them to remove paper jams. This was "explained" by virtue of the fact that stopping and restarting one of the huge presses would cause so much downtime and scrap that the performance standard would be impossible to achieve. This was a real dilemma, but it would become a problem only to an operator who paid attention to the sign.

Defense mechanisms are an important part of healthy human behavior. Being too open is just as problematic as being too closed, which is why T-groups and sensitivity training have had mixed results in industry. To strip people of their defenses and then return them to a culture that does not value openness is often asking for trouble.

The Japanese have developed a fascinating ritual that preserves their myths while creating the opportunity for accurate feedback. In spite of their innovative approaches to productivity, on-the-job criticism of management is not considered acceptable behavior. Instead, work groups will stop at a bar after work for a cup or two of sake. Here, employees are free to voice their dissatisfaction with current management practices. The next day they may sheepishly apologize for such behavior, blaming the influence of alcohol.

In contrast, our organizational culture encourages people to speak up. Indeed, we go to great lengths, through attitude surveys and opinion polls, to get people to "tell it like it is." When no corrective action is taken, we merely transform nagging dilemmas into full-blown problems.

Futility: Tilting at Windmills

A wise person is one who is wary of people—including managers and consultants—who have all the answers before a single question has been asked. However, one should be equally concerned with those who have all the questions but none of the answers.

One of the businesses I am in is conducting management seminars. A frequent excuse given by managers who do not attend is that their business will fall apart if they are not there every day. Sometimes I tell them that an equal concern may be that it won't. A valid response to my comment is to suggest that what I have to offer is perhaps of no value. The problem with all education is that it begins with answers before the questions have been asked. Taken together, we have a model for problems that are created by attempts to solve dilemmas for which there are no solutions.

An impossible dream is a dilemma that becomes a problem only when it is converted into an impossible goal (see Figure 4). If my goal is 100-percent attendance at my seminar, I have a problem. A salesperson who expects all prospects to become customers has the same problem. One of the myths of management is that asking for the impossible will get you more than if you ask for the possible. In fact, though, quite the opposite is true. The psychological concept of *goal gradient* demonstrates that the closer we get to a goal, the higher is our level of motivation to achieve it. When the goal is so distant as to be impossible, people may withdraw, become depressed, or even commit suicide.

Another way to deal with futility is to make the *process* of dreaming a goal in itself. The notion of getting an "A for effort" is a myth that resists the intrusion of reality. Indeed, a key source of frustration in management is the confusion between effort and productivity. Working smarter, not harder, is a slogan that violates the norms of most organizations.

In the seminar example, the *belief* that absence from work would cause disaster met that manager's need and thus provided his or her motivation. The fear of being proved wrong was so great that he or she could not take the chance. This explains much about why some people are able to snatch defeat out of the jaws of victory.

A variation on this theme is the expectation that accomplishing a goal will result in a problem-free state. Couples often divorce soon after the purchase of their dream house. Many managers of successful plant start-ups quit or are fired within a year after the new operation comes on stream. Reality is that the solution of a problem or the accomplishment of a goal merely creates the opportunity to handle a new one. It is significant enough to warrant a rule.

Rule 22: Growth is the creation of problems, not their elimination.

The most stressful time in a person's life is during a period of transition. The expectation that such a transition (say, marriage, childbirth, divorce, retirement) will result in a state of nirvana contributes to this stress.

In contrast to problems of denial, those of futility often result in blaming the behavior of others. For example, I may say that the reason why all managers don't come to my seminar is that they are stupid, which goes to prove how much they need it. This circular reasoning taken to the extreme is called *paranoia*, in which all problems are seen as caused by others. Solutions often involve crusades that seek to convert people to the "right" way of thinking. In a mild form, such behavior leads to the effort-performance dilemma. Take this example.

The Achilles Shoe Company had a number of jobs that were paid on a piece rate; standards were precisely set by the industrial engineering department, based on extensive time-and-motion study. One such job was that of sole cutter, a function that involves taking a rectangle of leather, cutting it to shape, turning, placing it on a hook attached to a moving belt, turning back, and cutting the next sole. The standard was set at 50 soles per hour. One employee, nicknamed "Harry the Hook," produced 100 per hour. Direct observation revealed Harry's secret: after cutting out the sole, he simply tossed it over his shoulder onto the hook. At the end of each hour he picked up his infrequent misses and hung them. Unlike fairy tales, Harry was severely admonished for goofing off.

The agony of problems of denial and futility is that the solution is not only worse than the problem, it *is* the problem. Focusing on how people should or shouldn't behave completely ignores the accomplishment of results.

One manager who did attend my seminar was a real star during the business games that are part of the course. At the end, he told me that he had cheated. Although his style throughout the course had been participative, he was in "real life" an autocrat. I answered that it didn't matter. My objective was for him to know *how* to be participative so that he could use that style in an appropriate situation. I then shared with him my first experience as a manager.

My assignment was to coordinate the dissemination of an employee opinion survey that had been conducted prior to my arrival. In two weeks, there were to be meetings with top management to discuss the results. All that remained was for the computerized report to be copied and sent to the printer for binding. In my first staff meeting, I was assured that everything was proceeding on course. As a show of my trust and "participative style," I did not push for details.

Two days before the meetings were to begin, the reports arrived, all 300 pages handsomely bound in imitation leather. As I flipped through one, I was shocked and dismayed to find that they were bound in random order. Page 1 was followed by page 39, followed by page 211, and so on. In a panic, I called my staff together.

The story unfolded as follows. Copies had arrived late on a Friday afternoon and were due to be picked up for binding at the end of the day. The task of collating was "delegated" to two secretaries. They quickly realized that it would be impossible to do in the time allotted, so they just made stacks of pages of equal height.

It was a long time before I could laugh at this painful memory, particularly when my boss told me that it would go down as a black mark in my record. I now cherish the whole affair as a valuable lesson in management. The stupidity and injustice of it have been overshadowed by my learning what happens in an organization that so values results that any result is seen as better than admitting defeat. The real sadness is that such organizations see themselves as tough competitors, when in fact they produce garbage. But then I may be so paranoid that I blame them for my failure as a manager.

Right and Wrong—Double Binds

Systems problems often involve situations in which people are damned if they do and damned if they don't. Such situations are a frequent cause of lose-lose conflict. For example, if you accuse people of being defensive, they are trapped: if they disagree, they are being defensive; if they agree, they are defensive by definition.

In a previous chapter, I described an absentee program in which the inclusion of a lottery ticket with weekly paychecks as a reward for perfect attendance resulted in significantly reduced overtime. Some managers, however, felt that the policy was "blackmail" and that people *should* come every day because it was the right thing to do.

One of the most difficult concepts for parents and managers to accept is that punishment does not produce lasting behavior change. The myth of "Spare the rod and spoil the child" is so deeply ingrained in our culture as to be unquestioned. And logic will not prevail in spite of all the evidence to the contrary. Plant rules are a good example. Invariably they will tell people what *not* to do, often adding the negative consequences of noncompliance.

Punishment is a double-bind dilemma that often results in a problem. The threat of punishment appears to deter people from acting wrongly. The threateners are not satisfied; they want people to act appropriately because it's right, not because of the threat. But they also fear that, without such threats, the person would quite "naturally" misbehave. It is an intrasystem dilemma that can be resolved only from the outside. Such problems often involve assumptions about human nature, which is why prejudice and bigotry between ages, sexes, races, and cultures will never be resolved from within the group. To break out of such binds one must escape the system. For similar reasons, organizational innovation most often takes place in new plants and factories, and even the introduction of a new player can produce substantial change. Here is an example.

Consolidated Conglomerates was a billion-dollar corporation that produced a 2 percent return on assets. It was literally worth more dead than alive. Everyone knew it was in some businesses that were draining the profits of its more successful divisions. The president continued to express his faith in these dogs in spite of their obvious misfit with the rest of the organization. When he retired, a new president was promoted from one of the more successful divisions. In his first staff meeting he announced, "Two-percent return is not acceptable, and I want a divestiture plan from each of you." Intrasystem change is often a result of blazing insight into the obvious.

On the other hand, extrasystem change is often unexplainable. Since the solution is often the problem, the problem can be solved by not trying to solve it. Like quicksand, the more you struggle to get free, the more you get stuck. Most parents know that the appropriate response to small children who threaten to leave home is to offer to help them pack their bags, while affirming their love and expressing how much the child will be missed. By not getting hooked into a battle of wills, the problem is avoided. It is the answer to Rule 19.

> *Rule 23:* The way to avoid crooked games is to choose
> not to play.

This does *not* necessarily mean one should pick up one's marbles and go home. Quitting is still playing the crooked game; there is no change. The challenge is to change the rules while keeping the ball in play. Thus, to "explain" poor performance as a bad attitude is to become locked into a game of attitude change where there can be no winner.

An alternative is to redefine the situation in terms of opportunity for improvement. There is even a logical arithmetic basis. A person who produces at 90 percent of standard has only 10 percent left to improve if the standard is tight. A person who produces at 50 percent of standard can improve by 5 times the amount of the first person. It is paradoxical that productivity improvement is more often directed at the "stars" who are already working near their limits, rather than the low performers who represent the major potential for increased output.

In his book *A Separate Reality*, Carlos Castaneda reports learning from Don Juan that "explaining" is a way of not seeing. This is the essence of Rule 1. Facts and fiction are only discernible in terms of our perceptions. To explain something is not necessarily to understand it. To understand people, one must know their dreams and values as well as their goals and norms. To understand a group or organization, one must focus on formal *and* informal structure. Reality is not defined by one or the other, but by both.

The same is true when defining problems. To really understand situations, one must know not only the symptoms (usually called "the problem"), but also the solutions that have been tried. The key, however, is to define *what must happen* in order that there be a resolution. Glass targets are hard to hit because you can't tell where the first bullet went. Attitudes are impossible to change because there is nothing to look at. There must be agreement as to what constitute's a bull's-eye (shattered glass, a cheerful smile, or whatever).

If the target can't be defined, it is a dilemma and not a problem. Leave it alone. Make a wind chime out of it. The problem of trying to hit a glass target is the trying, not the target. If you ask most people how to hit a glass target, they will tell you how to aim, where to stand, and a whole host of intrasystem suggestions. But actually, the way to hit glass targets is quite simple: paint them black.

As a final example, consider the task of teaching a child to ride a bicycle. If you are like most parents, you will run alongside as your son or daughter attempts to master balance and control. You hold on because you don't want your child to get hurt. Pain is avoided, but so is learning. The problem is that in order for most people to learn how to ride a bike, they have to fall off. That's what your kids do while you're at work. They don't tell you because they recognize that you are playing the game "good parent," and they don't want to hurt your feelings. That we learn from our mistakes is a dilemma because no one likes to make mistakes. The problem arises when we expect learning but won't tolerate error. It is a double bind of the worst sort.

In industry, the bicycle dilemma arises when we try to teach people how to run a machine. Logic dictates that we familiarize them with every nut, bolt, cog, and wheel. Then we put them "on line" with the warning not to screw up. As soon as the switch is thrown, learning ceases. The dilemma is that if the machine runs flawlessly, you don't need the operator. If it breaks down, the operator is not equipped to fix it because he or she was trained only to run it. The problem is that more and more training yields less and less results.

Two real solutions are possible. An extrasystem solution would be to teach operators to troubleshoot—that is, encourage them to experiment during training and then teach them how to correct the machine when the result is not acceptable. It is an illogical idea, but it works. This is the nature of extrasystem solutions. An alternative is to create an explicit troubleshooting chart and tape it to the machine. To be effective, it must assume that the operator has no mechanical ability. A simple "if this happens, try this" approach is best. Simplicity is the keystone of intersystem solutions.

Resistance to Change

I once saw a sign that read, "Don't get mad at me, I'm not trying to help you." It was love at first sight, but I didn't know why. As a professional "helper," I am often asked to rescue people from a dilemma. If I agree, they then seem to put all their energy into stopping me. This is called the "advice trap." If you take my advice and fail, it is my fault. If you succeed, you note that you would have taken that course anyway and my advice was superfluous. On a large scale, organizations play that game with respect to economic conditions. During boom times, success is attributed to good management. In times of hardship, it is the economy, not management, that is at fault.

The secret of dealing with resistance to change—to flow with the resistance rather than fight it—has been known by oriental cultures for centuries. Common sense suggests that problems of excessive optimism should be "solved" by pointing out flaws and those of pessimism by pep talks, but nothing could be further from the truth. The next time a salesperson comes in with a sales projection that rivals the parting of the Red Sea, nod your approval. Talk about gearing up production, adding another shift, buying more material. Like magic, the projection will begin to come back to earth. In like manner, if you suspect being "low-balled," talk about plant layoffs, shorter manufacturing hours, and perhaps discontinuing an item or two.

As for myself, I no longer resist giving advice. However, I do require a solemn pledge before I offer it: if I give it, the recipient must agree to take it regardless of the consequences. Rarely am I asked again.

Reference

Castaneda, Carlos, *A Separate Reality*. New York: Simon & Schuster, 1971.

11

Group Change

I hear you knocking but you can't come in.   Famous doorman

Chapter 2 opens with a story about a disillusioned new employee. When a new person enters a group both he *and* the group experience change. Imagine a circle of people tightly holding hands and an individual trying to break into the chain. The process is called "socialization," and it involves the transformation of a stranger into a member. The dynamics of a group fighting to maintain its orderly existence (Rule 4) and a stranger struggling to gain acceptance are prime examples of the group-change process. How a group deals with socialization will in large part determine how it will respond to change.

There is an additional rationale for groups to resist the entry of new members. It is based on the notion that the more difficult the joining process, the more valued will be the state of membership. Thus, the many rituals of initiation play an important part in maintaining the perceived value and continued survival of the group. The following is an extreme case in which a client company actually incorporated this dynamic into its hiring process.

Omega Office Product Systems was a pioneer in voice-actuated typewriters. It created the market and for a long time controlled it. Its dilemma was that the pipeline of hot-shot salespeople seemed to be drying up. The failure rate of recent sellers was excessive.

My initial discussions focused on OOPS's extensive battery of selection tests. Later, I asked to talk to the sales managers who did the actual hiring. What I learned was simply astounding.

Once a candidate passed the tests and interviews, he or she was not contacted further. Only those who were rejected received communication in the form of a polite refusal letter. The rationale was expressed by one manager who said, "We are the best. If they are really any good, they will beat down the door and demand an answer. That's when we hire them."

During the early years, this strategy worked very well. If a person wanted to sell a "voice writer," he or she had to go with OOPS. But times had changed. A number of foreign firms had further perfected the device and were selling it for less. In addition, they were aggressively recruiting sales personnel. Thus, the hotshots were turning away from the closed door in favor of the competition's red carpets.

The Entry Game

In Monopoly, every player starts out with equal chances and goes around and around the board until there is a winner. The structure is fixed by the board and the rules are clearly outlined on the cover. Thus, success would appear to be purely a function of luck. However, as pointed out in Chapter 8, this is true only if two robots are playing. Further, when more than two players are involved, the possibility of coalition opens up and negotiation skill becomes a critical factor.

Entry into a group is a similar game. To make it interesting, the game board is blank except for the edges defined by formal structure. You may be given a printed set of instructions (values), but you learn the rules (norms) as you go. Even the game room is significant: slogans and trophies suggest that the object of the game is to gain acceptance by proving loyalty. Of course, the skilled player knows the real objectives (goals) unfold only as the game is played.

This is not fantasy. One need only to recall the first day at school or work to relive the pressure and anxiety of being the new kid on the block. If you are lucky, a veteran will take pity on you and show you the ropes. Otherwise, you are on your own to figure out the locations of the gold mines as well as the land mines.

There is a television commercial in which a little boy is encouraged by his older brothers to try a new cereal. Told by their parents that it's good for them, they are quick to suspect its flavor, and they use "Mikey" as a guinea pig to find out how it tastes.

Street-wise kids know enough to be wary of anything that is advertised as "good." Proclamations by parents and teachers that school will be enjoyable are quickly dispelled by actual fact. So is the notion that work can be its own reward. These preconceptions of the newcomer add to the forces that act to retain the status quo.

What we really learn in school is the value of structure. Performance is measurable with constant feedback. Progress proceeds logically from grade to grade as if designed by Milton Bradley. There are even ceremonies to reward passing "Go."

The trap is that once high school is completed, the squares start to get fuzzy. The shock of college, despite all its apparent structure, is the reality that most of one's time is one's own; very little is controlled by others. No less a shock awaits those who enter the world of work. Training programs may prolong the event, but sooner or later people discover they are on their own. Without compass or map, they attempt to carve out a place for themselves.

Set adrift without the comfort of structure, we eagerly seek it from groups, which leads to the trade-off: our specific unique personal needs are bartered to gain entry. How we go about this process may very well determine the name of the game—as may the layout.

The Layout

Bank robbers, high divers, and stray dogs know enough to "case" a place before plunging in. "Casing" is also the stock in trade of consultants whose major skill, irrespective of technical expertise, is diagnosis. Quite simply, if you want to learn the management game you must learn how to diagnose. If all you study is the content, then you have learned nothing. (This is not a crime, mind you; indeed, a wise investor who is unwilling or unable to learn the intricacies of the stock market does well to stay out of it and hire a pro. The same advice, rarely taken, goes for managers. As a matter of fact, I have a consulting friend who engages only clients who let him run the show.) But for those who choose to play the hand, the following is a short course in diagnosis. The key elements are listed here:

Function	Content	Process	Variable
Role	Tasks	Image	Decision making
Authority	Title	Power	Leadership
Status	Formal structure	Informal structure	Communication
Identity	Internal perception	External perception	Values
Culture	Labels	Location	Norms

To illustrate, let us begin with the most basic group, the family. Roles are assigned on the basis of who does what. In the traditional family, such roles are consistent between *tasks*, such as the man's being the primary source of income, and his *image* as the "breadwinner." The woman's role is equally clear in terms of both task and image. Much has been written recently about families that are breaking up from such a tradition, particularly in relation to women's rights. In actual fact, throughout history tasks have been allocated across a wide spectrum of permutations—for example, there have always been families with female breadwinners. However, most of them maintained the *image* of tradition. It is the image that has changed in recent years as much as the facts.

The key factor is that of decision making. There is more than a grain of truth in the joke about the husband who makes the big decisions such as which political party to support and the wife who

makes the little decisions like where to live. Real role change, however, will not take place unless and until the process is altered such
that images and tasks become congruent. One woman at West Point
is worth a thousand marches on Washington. It is pictures, not
words, that will determine the outcome of the game.

A second but related function in groups is that of authority. The
trigger mechanism is power. As pointed out by Rule 9 (to gain
power, act as if you have it), power is a perceptual process and, as
such, is closely tied to image. Thus, the title of parent does little to
describe the power relationship between an adult and child. The
real determinant is style of leadership. It is worthy of more than
passing note that how a manager deals with his or her children will
largely reflect how that person handles subordinates. The groups
may be different in terms of tasks and titles but the process is the
same. To diagnose a family or a foundry, get a clear bead on image
and power. They will tell you about who makes the decisions and
where the leadership lies.

Status is a function that begins to get into the subtleties of
group games. The key variable is communication. In families, the
arena is often the dinner table. It is perhaps the only time the whole
group is together in one place. The rules governing who sits where
and does what present a microcosm of the formal and informal
structures. In the movie *Life With Father*, just one scene is enough
to convey that there is a benevolent autocrat at the helm.

The work group equivalent to the dinner table is the meeting.
It takes attendance at only a few to begin to get a clearer picture of
how the game board is structured. Like John in Chapter 2, it is often
where those who go in blind get their eyes opened.

The identity of a group is always easier to see from the outside
than from within. As discussed in Chapter 8, the process of group
formation includes a natural distortion of values that can lead to
conflict. A family's values can often be discerned by the life style it
chooses. For example, children have little concept of rich and poor;
humorist Sam Levinson often told the story of how he never knew

his family was poor because his mother kept a tin can for spare pennies to be sent to those less fortunate than they were.

Value itself is a relative term that has no meaning beyond some arbitrary comparison. Thus, the identity of a group is a function of some other group or groups. What becomes significant, then, is the *basis* for comparison rather than the comparison itself. That families are most often compared by socioeconomic status suggests why so many play the game of "keeping up with the Joneses."

Another aspect of identity is the phenomenon of "I know, you know I know, and I know that you know that I know"—secrets that are common knowledge but are not discussed openly. Families in particular have these sacred cows, which are tolerated by pretending that they don't exist.

Lastly, there is the function of group culture, which is perhaps the most difficult to define clearly. The culture of a group is so ingrained in its norms that only by paying attention to apparently minor details does its full impact become apparent. Like defining identity, one is left with abstractions unless there is some basis for comparison to other groups. Culture determines habit and is thus unusual only when it differs from our own.

My initial exposure to this notion occurred the first time I ordered meat loaf outside my parents' home. When the waiter placed the slice of neatly formed ground beef on my plate, I politely requested that he give me one that had a slice of hard-boiled egg in the center. In response, I got the blankest of stares. It finally dawned on me that some people may not prepare the dish the way my mother does. To this day, I can't enjoy the strange way "outsiders" cook meat loaf.

The process issue that relates to culture is location—where people physically position themselves when the group is together. Who sits at the head of the table, gets the most comfortable chair, and drives the car on trips gives significant clues within family groups. In organizations, the prized locations tend to be corner offices and reserved parking spaces. Although not discussed openly, these are jealously guarded symbols of a person's position.

Identity and culture are vital to defining layout because they are "border issues" that differentiate the group from the rest of the populace. So much of our environment is so homogeneous that we often overlook these variables until we sit in the wrong seat and get those funny stares.

The Play

The dynamics of an individual's interaction with a group are determined not only by the layout but also by the players. The dimensions of play are a function of people's level of conformity and flexibility. Conformity is the degree to which the group is able to change the individual; the extreme opposite of conformity is heresy. Flexibility is the *perceived* amount of change an individual assumes he or she can bring about in a group; it is a process of bending but not breaking. Inflexibility is labeled with a whole host of adjectives ranging from "stubborn" to "high-principled," depending on the referee.

Taken together, we have four basic player styles in games of change. They are:

1. flexible conformity
2. inflexible conformity
3. flexible heresy
4. inflexible heresy

Note that nothing has been said about the specific nature of the group nor the personality of the individual. Once again, it really doesn't matter. The group's goal is to hold tight and the individual's is to get in. The process is the same in a factory or a fraternity. The play will determine the issues of change.

Politics is a strategy of flexible conformity. Rules are well known, and they are often bent to their limits. However, the individual changes as much as the "system" in the process. In contrast, inflexible conformity is a strategy in which the player will not yield on specific goals. Such is the nature of entrepreneurship. Indeed, the most common reason people give for starting their own business is an unwillingness to work for someone else.

Flexible heresy is a process in which the individual takes what he or she can get from a group. Though quick to change goals, the individual's strategy remains fixed. Flexible heresy is exemplified by the "yes man" who so needs group membership that he is unable to take a stand.

Inflexible heresy is the mark of a dictator or extreme autocrat. Goals are cast in concrete and any strategy will be employed to achieve them. It is often sung to the tune of "the end justifies the means."

A Game of Change

To further illustrate the preceding concepts, let us take an in-depth look at a group trying to cope with change. As is usually the case, some event has caused the group to become unbalanced. In the following example, the superintendent of the Rockfish Central School District had issued an edict that the staff-support departments must operate as a team. The group consisted of the directors of the four service departments: psychology, social work, speech and hearing, and health.

Tom was the Director of Psychological Services. Young and aggressive, he tried to exert considerable influence over the group. It was immediately apparent that he felt his profession was more valuable than those of the other three.

Dick, who was in charge of the social workers, was a man of about 60 whose title was Associate Director of Support Services. (It was significant to note that the group's boss once held this position and was himself trained as a social worker.) Dick was the number-two man in the organization.

Harriet was the Director of Speech and Hearing for the school district. She was a dynamic middle-aged woman who was the undisputed informal leader of the group.

Madelaine was in charge of the school nurses and directly reported to the County Director of Public Health. A quiet unassuming woman, she came to meetings dressed in her nurse's uniform.

Diagnosis

One of the rarely discussed theoretical issues about work groups is the physical location of people. Yet it is vital to know the layout in order to understand the game. It was particularly critical in this case, as the two women did not have permanent offices but rather "floated" from school to school. The men, on the other hand, had offices in the main administration building. Thus, there was the potential for male-female as well as for office-field conflict. However, such conflict was prevented by the lack of coalition within the pairs. Tom resented that Dick was second in command and, although their offices were next to each other, they rarely cooperated. Harriet did not see Madelaine as a comrade and preferred to fight the "boys" on her own. Madelaine contributed to this lack of coalition by emphazing that her reporting relationship was external to the school system; in actual fact, she was an employee of the Public Health Department, not of the Department of Education.

The next result was a "four-cornered" game in which each department functioned independently with little coordination or cooperation. Such games are typical of professional rivalries where task supersedes function.

It was apparent from the start that the group did not function as a team. Indeed, it made no attempt even to pretend that such was the case. Score was kept on the basis of "head count"—that is, the number of pupils treated during a school year. Each department kept its own score. Each viewed the others as competition for head count. The superintendent's problem was the tremendous overlap of services. The issue for the groups was that staffing levels were computed on the basis of number of pupils served. Thus, their survival depended on that count. This dilemma became a problem with the issuance of the team edict.

Since this was an extragroup problem (everyone was satisfied until the superintendent instituted the team), change would most likely result from fiddling more with the layout than with the players. Five choices were possible, each corresponding to one of the functions outlined in the table earlier in this chapter. They were:

1. Change roles by holding all groups accountable for pupil decisions.
2. Change authority by centralizing power in one person.
3. Change status by restructuring the organization into a single hierarchy.
4. Change identity by reducing emphasis on professions.
5. Change culture by locating groups together physically.

The trigger mechanism would have to be the score-keeping system. Without common goals, the group rightly saw joint problem solving as a waste of time.

Intervention

As mentioned previously, the nature of extrasystem change is its apparent illogic. While an inside person would quite rationally make some direct push for cooperation (which is what the superintendent did), my strategy as an outsider was quite the opposite. It was to first clarify the situation by intensifying the pain rather than by applying some soothing balm.

In our first session, I asked the players to write out the condition under which a student should be referred to them. They were then to read their analysis to the group. Predictably, each department felt that all pupils should start with its particular area of expertise. As openness and trust developed in the group, each was able to admit that its being the referring department would guarantee its credit for a child's treatment.

To be able to admit this was quite risky, as the values of the organization were directed at the children's welfare not the departments'. Thus, to bring about change the group had to come face to face with Rule 1. It is axiomatic that those in the helping professions have the greatest difficulty learning it. It bears repeating.

> *Rule 1:* People always act in their own best interest,
> given the facts as they know them.

The brief written exercise changed the "facts." Since everyone was playing the reference game by headcount, they recognized the tremendous waste of resources. They began to see there was no real advantage to continuing *if* the others ceased as well. Thus, the groundwork was laid for a problem-solving approach to change—to create a win-win solution by defining the problem accurately. Here, then, was the problem as they outlined it for the superintendent:

> The support-services function does not possess a centralized referral source. Since each department is separately accountable for pupils, each operates as its own clearing house. This is at the core of the overlap dilemma.

This, of course, was the content definition, the one for public consumption. The process definition went like this:

> We are caught in a potential zero-sum game in which we cannot risk the loss of head count by having other departments control referrals. The separate score-keeping system is at the core of the overlap dilemma.

Once defined, the group was able to quickly move toward a solution. The medium was the "annual report." Every year, each department was required to submit a summary of its activities and services to the superintendent. With his concurrence, the report that year was a joint effort that resulted in one document. It became a focal point for continued team development. The ultimate winners, of course, were the children who no longer had to have their temperature taken before being referred for psychological evaluation. Likewise, a hearing test was no longer a prerequisite for the treatment of family problems.

Conclusions

Purists may argue that a whole host of problems were not dealt with in this case. If so, they have missed the point. The remaining conflicts are *dilemmas* not problems. The imbalance was caused by the superintendent's proclamation. The joint annual report restored that balance. By altering support services' image and the process by which decisions were made, the role of director changed as it related to referrals. Authority, status, identity, and culture remained the same. Since those types of changes involve the whole organization, they will be dealt with in the next chapter.

12

Organizational Change

Into every life a little rain must fall.

Famous umbrella salesman

Organizations exist to survive (Rule 6). But often, an organization's survival depends on forces outside its structural boundaries. So much has been written about how to change organizations that one might assume it to be an initiating process. It is not. Change almost always happens as a *reaction* to an undesirable state. Just as groups fight to maintain order, so organizations struggle to stay afloat in an environment that by nature is unpredictable.

Change occurs when the pain of the current situation exceeds the price of changing or when the need for change is much greater than the pain. Thus, change always involves risk. The process of reducing risk is that of control. The fundamental issue for managers of organizations is not the creation of change but the control of it.

Risk

Economic growth can occur only through innovation. But to be creative is to increase risk. The notion that a manager in an organization is a risk taker is mostly myth. Indeed, some management advice givers go so far as to suggest that decisions never be made unless they are absolutely necessary. This is why entrepreneurs have no place in traditional organizations. They want to shoot craps in a house dedicated to clipping coupons.

Because organizations can survive the loss of any one member (Rule 5), the impact of the individual is often perceived to be insignificant. In a bit of chicken-egg circularity, the system creates an environment that punishes, rather than rewards, further creativity. Soon it cannot attract those who would continue the process of growth or change. The net result is a major change in the game. While the objective of an entrepreneur is to win, the goal of a traditional organization is to reduce risk. On a logical basis, risk reduction makes a lot of sense. Psychologically, however, it is a losing strategy. Like a giant casino, inflation and competition "grind out" organizations that fail to increase productivity through change.

The dilemma is that no organization can become big or secure enough to ignore the possibility that another may introduce innovations so significant that the former will cease to exist. The problem is that such organizations do not understand the process of change. Risk reduction becomes a *passive* strategy that attempts to prevent things from happening. This is the essence of bureaucracy: gambling cannot be tolerated and individuals cannot be held accountable for results.

The result of this dilemma and problem is that there is no control. In extremes cases success and failure become pure outcomes of chance.

Control

Organization implies control by its nature. Processes of control aim to contain individual behavior in an effort to maintain order. Given all the internal and external forces acting on organizations the issue of control versus conformity creates a significant dilemma in that human needs require freedom to act while values and norms seek to limit that freedom. The real problem, however, is in the process itself—in other words, *how* control is exercised.

Control is an emotionally charged concept that is significantly influenced by the wants and needs of individuals. Often it is perceived to be synonymous with manipulation. This is dandy for folks who want to be nurtured, but it wreaks havoc on those who are trying to achieve some degree of self-actualization.

The bottom line is that much of the control dilemma relates to the issue of evaluation of performance or, more specifically, the threats and punishments associated with not performing. Since the purpose of control is to achieve goals, it *should* have some impact on performance. That it so often doesn't provides a great deal of support for abandoning the traditional process. Indeed, most managers studiously avoid such tasks as performance appraisal anyway.

The heart of the matter is that the traditional concept of control, with its assumptions of power and authority, just doesn't fit. The opportunity to fool around with irrelevant behavior while performance goes to hell in a basket is too great. The content aspect of control, however, is valid. Since a manager's role is to achieve desired results (Rule 7), the function of control is to make that happen. The process, then, is to verify, check, and provide feedback while moving toward goals. It is the creation of a set of standards against which performance can be measured. Without measurable standards of performance, there can be no basis for feedback. This is why organizations single out communication as their most significant problem. It is the lack of feedback, inherent in communication dilemmas, that yields poor control. In more stable times this results in merely drifting along. With accelerated change, though, come more opportunities to go under. The challenge for management, therefore, is twofold: first, to accurately diagnose the organization; second, to build in controls.

Organizational Diagnosis

There are perhaps as many theories of what to look at in organizations as there are theorists. Too often, however, such hypotheses appear to be written more for other theorists than for the managers

Figure 13. Organizational anchors.

who need to use them. The result is a proliferation of complex systems diagrams that confuse more than clarify.

Organizational diagnosis really involves three basic issues: purpose, goals, and barriers. These translate into knowing what business you are in, having a clear fix on measurable goals, and sharply defining problems and dilemmas. These points are diagramed in Figure 13. Note that these variables are not connected. They are anchor points from which a position can be fixed. Each is defined by the other two. Thus, a barrier only has meaning in terms of the purpose and goal it separates. To connect purpose and goal, we must add a fourth variable: action, or some movement from purpose to goal. Such movement includes both action taken and action anticipated. When such action is controlled, it is said to follow a plan; when undirected, it is history, culture, or both.

Figure 14. Organizational diagnosis.

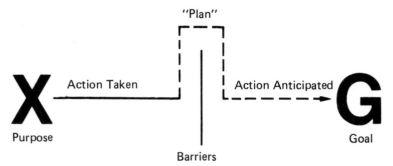

Organizational diagnosis must include such action in order to complete the picture. As mentioned in the previous chapter, problems are often best defined by the solutions attempted rather than the situation itself. This is illustrated in Figure 14. With the addition of the "plan," we have a schematic for diagnosing an organization accurately. We know where it is, where it is going, what stands in its way, and how it hopes to get there. It does not, however, take change into account. Because purpose, goals, and barriers are in constant motion there is the need for some process that monitors such movement. Indeed, such feedback mechanisms are the essence of *controlled* change. That is Rule 24.

Rule 24: Feedback is the key to controlling change.

Effective management means facing choices and making them. The skill involved requires managers to know what needs to change, where they must intervene, and how to bring the change about. The nuts and bolts of the process are most obvious in turnaround situations.

A Case of Turnaround

It happens so often and with such similarity that it's almost ritualistic: an organization's performance slides into mediocrity and management appears helpless in trying to reverse the trend. Finally, in desperation, the person at the top is replaced. As if by magic, the new person begins to change the course of events and a turnaround is soon accomplished. Indeed, an improvement is often seen immediately with no change other than that of the top manager. Of course, such performance jumps are short-lived unless other steps are taken. The rationale for this is at the heart of controlling change.

Managers of an ailing organization are reluctant to change their process because to do so would be an admission that their previous efforts had resulted in failure. The longer and harder they pound away with ineffective strategies, the more committed they become to proving themselves right. But when the axe falls, you can almost hear their sigh of relief. In addition, the mere act of change is a signal to the organization that all is not well.

Most top executives are so inbred that, by the time they work their way through the system, they can only see what others before them have seen. Thus, when an "outsider" moves in (from another division or another company), he or she is able to respond immediately to different perceptions. The following is one such case.

The Pompano Powder Works was constructed two years ago and was awash in red ink. Located in central Florida, it was built to replace an antiquated operation in the Midwest. The parent corporation was disgusted with PPW's performance to the point of contemplating its closing. As a last resort, I was called in to assess whether a turnaround was possible. Needless to say, the current management was less than thrilled by my arrival. Although my area of expertise is process, a number of content issues were identified as significant.

First, the old plant was a "batch" operation. Gunpowder was made in tubs, and experienced supervisors often tested the product by tasting it; yes, they literally put it in their mouths to determine the proper mix of ingredients. The new plant was a "chemical process" operation where product flowed through ductwork on a continuous basis. Developed in the lab, it was the first full-scale operation of its type.

Second, the transfer of supervisors to Florida had been voluntary. Many of the top hands chose not to go and found work elsewhere.

Third, although the objective of the plant was to remain nonunion, cards were being passed out in an effort to get the required majority to hold an election. Supervisors did not oppose such a move; the old plant had been unionized and they were more comfortable with that process.

Finally, two incidents that occurred during my first visit reinforced my growing suspicion that management was trying to put a round peg in a square hole. One of the truck drivers who delivered raw product to the plant mentioned to me that this procedure was wasteful. He pointed out that being so far from the city and having so much acreage available, the company could more efficiently bring in such material by rail car; a covered hopper could be left on the company's siding and emptied as needed. (The Midwest plant had been located close to a major city and had had very little storage space available, and the old habits prevailed.)

Gunpowder being readied for shipment was stored in bunkers and the back lot was covered with craters dug for this purpose. As I toured this lot with the groundkeeper, he expressed his concern over the effects of a heavy rain. A native of the area, he pointed out that water would not run off quickly after a storm and that the craters would fill up and stay full for days. Further, he pointed out that there were a variety of poisonous snakes that would seek the high ground of the bunkers during such a storm. Sure enough, after a veritable monsoon a few months later, the managers found not only that the powder couldn't be kept dry but that it was being "protected" by a nest of vipers.

The preceding events were not totally unexpected; most plant start-ups are exercises in catastrophe. But there were two unique confounding factors: a process that had never been field-tested and the total disregard for the cultural differences between the old and the new plants. An unchanged structure was laid on a situation that cried out for doing things differently.

To top it off, the game wasn't even being played with the first team. The best managers and supervisors had preferred to find other employment rather than leave their Midwestern homes. What I discovered in Florida was what most turnaround managers find: a confused, undercontrolled operation that was floundering in quicksand. Every move it made just got it into deeper trouble. The current plant manager had given up and was waiting for someone to put him out of his misery. He didn't have much longer to wait. He was a good man, but not for that situation.

The new plant manager was selected on the basis of his track record with chemical plants, not because of any experience in the munitions business. It was he who eventually solved the problems of producing product on a continuous basis. Indeed, the corporation eventually transferred the Pompano Powder Works out of the Ammunition Division and into the Chemical Division, which represented a better fit. The new manager also made a special point of visiting customers to determine what they wanted and what they didn't want. He "used" his lack of product knowledge to have these people teach him the business. The result was insight that an old pro might never have gotten. At last, someone had figured out what business PPW was in. It was an important first step.

The new manager's next move was to shut down the plant for a week to train the people in how to run it. In plant start-ups that do not come on stream as scheduled, it is axiomatic that people are trained on the run. That is, not only are they required to learn to operate a piece of machinery, but they are also expected to produce to standard during their training. This behavior is a holdover from previous eras when a person was a "helper" for many years until he or she slowly acquired the knowledge and expertise to move up. Such luxury is not often available in new plants.

Once people were trained, the new manager turned his attention to the issue of quality. The manager of quality control was the best in the business when it came to technical expertise, but he also rejected most of the gunpowder that was produced. The plant manager changed this by holding him responsible for quantity as well as quality. That is, he could no longer merely stand at the door and be a policeman. Instead, he was forced to work with the production organization to make it right the first time.

Finally, intergroup conflict was addressed. As the plant had sunk deeper and deeper, each department began to blame the others for the company's misfortune. The plant manager clearly outlined a set of goals that he wished to achieve and for which he would hold all managers *equally* accountable. It took nearly a year, but the Pompano Powder Works did turn around and now produces at the levels for which it was designed.

It should be pointed out, however, that the new plant manager in this example faced a different set of risks than his predecessor did. Since he had no investment in the two years of futility and frustration, the original failure was not his. Thus, he had everything to lose and nothing to gain by retaining the status quo. Furthermore, he was able to diagnose the situation (with some help) and to build in controls. He did not change everything, only altering those functions that would have the greatest impact. He drew an invisible line on the scoreboard as if to say, "Everything prior to my arrival is history, now let's work together to get from point A to point B. I will show you how but the success will be yours." Like Franklin Roosevelt, the turnaround manager offers people a new deal. It is a strategy that works often and well.

Managing Change

There are no pat formulas for keeping an organization on top, but there is enough similarity in process to provide a framework for managing change effectively. These processes include:

Action mode
Simple structure
Improvement of productivity
Autonomy
Singleness of purpose
Loose-tight control
Customer contact

But strategy alone will not produce excellence. If it did, we could hire company presidents right out of business school. What is lacking is the experience and judgment to know where, when, and how to intervene in an organization. Management is a process of tuning and fiddling with the system until it sounds right. Simplistic as it seems, it is difficult to do. One must know what a well-tuned organization sounds like and how to detect when it is going off key. It is an action mode rather than a strategic one. Plans are rough drafts to be refined at the keyboard, but theorists try to write the whole symphony from scratch.

To achieve results, effective managers try to keep structure simple and emphasize a few well-defined goals. These goals are action-oriented, intended to fix the wheel and get it rolling rather than redesign it.

By emphasizing a singleness of purpose (what business you are in) and providing the autonomy to solve problems in entrepreneurial ways, effective organizations learn to *proact* rather than react to change. In spite of the accelerating rate of such change, the early warning signals are almost always evident to those who choose to see them. Technological innovation takes years to reach fruition, so surprises are almost nonexistent. The problem is most often a corporate bureaucracy that waits too long. And sometimes it is a hot product that is pushed from above without the support of the folks who have to make it and sell it. Junkyards are loaded with products pushed through by managements in spite of warnings from their own technical people. Corporate history is equally full of well-documented cases of the handwriting's being on the wall when no one was reading. It is the essence of being a day late and a dollar short.

Loose-Tight Controls

Although a seemingly contradictory term, loose-tight controls form the basis of controlled change. Indeed, they are the antidote to the dilemma of hierarchical structure.

Hierarchy, you may recall, was designed for military operation. An effective army is often described as functioning like a well-oiled machine, and in fact, the more machinelike the process, the more effective the structure. Control is based on the automatic nature of following orders and going by the book. Unfortunately such a process rarely works in business and industry. The rules are not clear enough and they keep changing.

An effective manager in such organizations does not control; rather, he or she develops the *process* of control through feedback mechanisms. The essential skill is knowing where to be tight and where to be loose. It is known as delegation—not the delegation of tasks (as is so often done), but the delegation of responsibility. The difference separates the players from the kibitzers.

Customer Service

All organizations have customers, even those who only serve themselves (in which case they are their own customers). Inherent in knowing what business you are in is knowing who your customers are and what they want. It is not coincidence that almost every new turnaround manager is quick to hit the road and talk to the people who pay the bills. Partly, of course, this is often a ploy to smooth the ruffled feathers caused by late shipments, poor service, and unacceptable quality. But it also serves the need for the kind of data only a user can provide.

Customer contact is a major way for an organization to see changes in time to respond. The irony is that so few managers do it—not the perfunctory "How are we doing?" (which translates to "Please tell us how wonderful we are"), but the probing questions that generate answers you may find painful to hear. In fact, the more they hurt, the more you need them. Although the marketplace isn't a fairy tale, it comes close to being one. Justice is almost always served when customer needs are not met.

Conclusions

Joe Hopkins was the manager of a multimillion-dollar plant that employed thousands of people. He had held his job for nearly ten years. Above his desk was a string of red lights, each one connected to a machine out on the floor. When a machine "went down," a light began to flash. It was a rare day when one didn't.

Because of petty pilferage, Joe installed a lock on the door to the small kitchen that housed the coffeepot. Keys were issued to managers only. Unauthorized coffee drinking stopped.

Day in and day out Joe "squeezed" his organization in an effort to get it under control. The more he squeezed, the more performance declined. Cost reduction after cost reduction brought about only temporary relief from plummeting profits. Finally, when the ink turned red, Joe was replaced.

Lest one be quick to criticize, it should be pointed out that for most of his career, Joe was a star. He did not change, but the situation did. Older equipment and younger workers created problems that he was not prepared to solve.

The above story is true and recurs over and over in organizations. Unfortunately, the real criminals are not the Joes of the world but their management, who leave them too long in a game that has changed. In baseball, when a pitcher gets "shelled," he takes a shower and shares the loss with his manager. In business, the player often gets the full blame while the top manager is rarely questioned about his or her culpability.

Before anything else, the most significant skill a manager can bring to the table is the ability to put the right person in the right job. Of course, in order to do so one must know how to play the game. Not that one must play it well, only that one know *how* it should be played.

Change starts outside an organization's boundaries. Problems begin at the bottom of an organizational hierarchy, not at the top. To anticipate change and to solve problems early, talent on the firing line is necessary. If an organization lacks such talent, it should seriously consider replacing its people with robots. The unique advantage of human beings is their ability to adapt. Managers who fail to grasp this point will always be playing from weakness rather than from strength.

It is fitting that a military man, General George C. Marshall, said it best. He argued that when a man working for him did not succeed, he assumed the fault was in the assignment and it was changed. If the man failed a second time, the general made the same assumption. Only after a third failure would he conclude that perhaps the army was not a suitable career for his subordinate.

PART V

MANAGEMENT

The buck stops here.   Famous doe

13

Competence

When you are up to your ass in alligators, it is difficult to remember your objective was to drain the swamp.   Famous dredger

A fundamental lesson that we all learn as children is to discount what people say but place great store in what they do. Adult life, to a child, is a seemingly endless series of contradictions. We say honesty is the best policy and then brag how we cheated the IRS. We argue for law and order but rarely obey speed limits. We rant and rave about drug abuse yet ingest large quantities of caffeine, nicotine, and alcohol.

Children are an adaptable lot and as part of their maturation process they accept all of this nonsense as part of being an adult. Indeed, in an effort to be grown-up they learn that what one says need neither be true nor make sense. Thus, their "explanations" for physical events such as monsters living under the bed and invisible friends in the closet seem no less illogical than our adult fairy tales.

One adult fairy tale centers on the issue of competence. Judging by how we treat it, one could easily assume that levels of skill are predetermined by genes and chromosomes because we judge people by what they do rather than what they accomplish. We seem to care more about behavior than results. Perhaps it begins with the parental admonition, "Behave yourself." In any event, what exists as a frustrating dilemma for children becomes a full-blown problem for adults in organizations. Playing by the rules becomes more important than winning.

A Historical Perspective

From prehistoric forest to corporate jungle, humans have continued to exist because of their ability to adapt to an ever changing environment. The one common thread throughout the historical tapestry of the world of work has been the issue of competence.

In the beginning, competence and survival were inexorably linked. The hunter was rewarded with fresh meat and the farmer with a bountiful crop. Incompetence led to starvation and death. Man* was accountable only to himself and his family, and his motivation was simple and direct. Working at the subsistence level, he was at the same time the producer and the consumer of his own output.

Man's adaptation at the time of the Industrial Revolution included the development of a new breed of worker—the manager. This development created a monumental dilemma that still remains unresolved. Without direct control over the standards of production, the manager must nonetheless evaluate the competence of his organization. In a sense he is "flying blind" and must rely on instruments to guide him. All too often these instruments fail to be calibrated to an accurate standard, and the organization fails to respond to his control. The results may range from a loss of profits to a failure to survive.

In the industrial renaissance of the eleventh century, some 700 years before the Industrial Revolution, the enslaved artisan was emancipated and became the master of his own workshop. Initially,

---

*Although I have tried to eliminate sexist language in this historical review, the roles in question have been traditionally "male."

he carried out all business functions; he was the workman, the merchant, and the shopkeeper.

In spite of his new-found freedom, his control over the quality of his product was less than complete. No longer was he the sole judge of his competence. The emergence of a mercantile economy created a new force to contend with, the consumer.

The role of the consumer has grown significantly from that humble beginning. And in the past decade or so, the consumer movement has become a powerful force that has resulted in major changes in the business world. The addition of numerous items of safety equipment to the automobile is a most obvious example. Contrary to what many believe, change has not been limited to the area of product design. At least one major automobile manufacturer, responding to public pressure over the issue of product quality, now includes detailed instructions in the owner's manual on how to register a complaint that cannot be answered at the dealer level.

The thrust of consumerism includes corrective pressures in the areas of defective materials, sloppy workmanship, and poor service. Thus, consumers are insisting on competence at all levels of industrial organizations. It is of particular importance to note that the increasing power of the consumer to control the quality of output has been a reaction to industry's failure to set and control its own standards of excellence.

Pressure for change is also evident in the concern over ecological destruction and environmental control. Our population has become sensitive to the issues of dirty air, stream pollution, excessive noise levels, the improper use of pesticides, and destruction of forests and other natural resources. The environmentalists have already amassed enough power to produce major changes. For example, they stopped the SST project even though its development was well under way, and they have required the automobile industry to clean up the exhaust emissions of its engines. Although many design changes have been stimulated, many more will be necessary before standards that will be enforced by law later in this decade can be met. Environmental action has led to the establishment of such strong antipollution laws that at least one major plant has been forced to close its gates permanently after having survived for more than 100 years. Often changes have been less dramatic, but they have been costly. Plants that formerly discharged heavy smoke, noxious gases, and particulate matter from their stacks have had to install combustion controls, precipitators, and other expensive equipment.

In addition to environmental control, other rules have been added to the game. The Equal Employment Opportunity Act of 1964 established standards and controls for hiring practices. The Occupational Safety and Health Act of 1970 is another example. And there is a strong likelihood that new controls will be established with increasing frequency. The net result may be that organizations will find that they cannot afford the price and will not survive. It has become apparent that those organizations that possess the resources and the flexibility to adapt to change are also the ones with the highest standards. Thus, the issue of competence once again becomes the key to survival.

Standards

In the Middle Ages, a craftsman seeking admission to the association of masters had to produce a sample of his skill—the *masterpiece*. Thus, a standard of excellence—tangible proof of competence—was expected. It had shape and texture. You could reach out and touch it.

During this same period, the craft guild came into being. The forerunner of the trade union, the guild was formed to serve a number of purposes. One of its most important functions, as attested by its extensive rules on the subject, was to set standards and thus ensure competence in a particular craft. For perhaps the first time, the free craftsman had more than just his own conscience as a guide for setting standards. Someone was looking over his shoulder to ensure that he did indeed produce a quality product.

Several centuries later, the industrial man was born in the hell holes of British cotton mills. Hunger and famine drove him from the fields and into the jaws of the Industrial Revolution. The link between competence and survival became less clear. Man was removed from the visual verification of his skill. Money and machines drove a wedge between the worker and his craft. Some became managers of people and administrators of paper. Unable to set standards or control quality directly, they searched for devices to expand their reach.

Scientific Management

Frederick Winslow Taylor proposed a system to increase productivity based on a "scientific" approach. It was his firm conviction that the goals of an individual and those of the organization are one and the same. His approach called for standards of performance and for regulations and procedures for every job. Work was reduced to laws, rules, and formulas.

Convinced that workers would respond to economic reward, Taylor never bothered to validate his hypothesis. Thus, what might have been loosely conceived as management never met the most minimal of criteria for being scientific.

Frank and Lillian Gilbreth tried a different approach. By studying the motions involved in bricklaying, they derived a system for improving the efficiency of production. Their major contribution was not the system itself but their belief that the details of the work situation should be adjusted to the individual rather than vice versa. Theirs was certainly a more realistic approach than Taylor's, but it breaks down very quickly when applied to a job that does not closely resemble bricklaying.

While modern management has gone well beyond these early beginnings of industrial engineering, it still places considerable emphasis on reason and logic. The resounding result of such approaches has been a failure to achieve the desired results. The typical manager, accustomed to using logic to arrive at successful approaches, generally rationalizes failure with some comment, often unprintable, about the perversity of human nature. For such a manager, this is an end point from which he or she either seeks solace or turns to other matters. But the truly rational, scientific approach to a formula that will not balance is to consider the possibility that at least one relevant variable has been overlooked.

Performance Appraisal

In a 1957 article, Douglas McGregor took what he called "An Uneasy Look at Performance Appraisal." He recommended that managers move away from judgments about behavior and focus on the achievement of objectives. And in 1965, Meyer, Kay, and French were forced to conclude that while most people think performance appraisal is a good idea, few can cite examples of constructive action—or significant improvement—that it achieves. Their study pointed to the questionable value of annual performance appraisals in that:

— Criticism has a negative effect on achievement of goals.
— Praise has little effect one way or the other.
— Performance improves most when specific goals are established.
— Defensiveness resulting from critical appraisal produces inferior performance.
— Coaching should be a day-to-day, not a once-a-year, activity.
— Mutual goal setting, not criticism, improves performance.
— Interviews designed primarily to improve a person's performance should not simultaneously weigh his or her salary or promotion in the balance.
— Participation by the employee in the goal-setting procedure helps produce favorable results.

Goals—The Missing Link

The issue of competence remains a dilemma because we have tried to put standards on *how* a task is done rather than on *what* results are achieved. Yet at the highest levels of the organization, the expectation of measurable results is very evident in operating plans and in the long-range business plan. These objectives can and must be tied to department, section, subsection, and individual goals.

Because it is difficult to translate operating plans into specific individual goals, the process of appraisal becomes crucial, not as a device for criticism but as a tool for negotiation between a manager and his or her subordinate *before* work is to be done. The key areas to be covered are:

— Goals: What must I accomplish?
— Time frame: When must I accomplish these goals?
— Priorities: Which are most critical?
— Standards: How will you measure my results?
— Values: What results must I achieve to rate a gold star? a silver star? a purple heart?

Some managers may balk at this process, arguing that the constantly changing organizational environment prohibits this kind of planning. Yet the alternative is to have no plan at all—or worse still, to have elegant programs, sophisticated technology, and highly educated people, but fail to survive.

The primary objective of any enterprise is to survive (Rule 6). This is a cold, hard reality. The Edsel was, by most automotive standards, an acceptable vehicle—but so what? In 1948, a car was developed that was exceptional even by today's standards, but few ever remember its name (the Tucker). The end may not justify the means, but it will determine the results—and that's what people will remember long after the behavior is forgotten.

Management and Science

Science is the acquisition of knowledge through study and observation. The failure of scientific management has been that the wrong thing was studied. The subject of competence leads one to observe behavior, which can be a dead end that equates success with effort.

Every schoolchild knows that studying hard does not guarantee a good grade; indeed, some do very well without ever opening a book. The real issue is performance. Somehow this lesson gets lost in organizations, perhaps because all that behavior is out there just waiting to be studied. More likely, though, the message is overlooked because it appears fairer that effort be directly rewarded. Thus, the fairy tale of the work ethic lives on. Managers continue to cry out in newspapers and magazines that people don't want to work hard anymore. When, oh when, will they learn that the only reward for sweat is greater profits for the manufacturers of deodorants?

A wise manager is one who knows the facts as well as the myths that surround the game. In an effort to impart a bit of that wisdom, the following section will attempt to resolve once and for all the behavior-performance dilemma.

Productivity

Productivity is a very sound scientific concept that is measured by the ratio of output to input. It takes a finite number of person-hours to produce a given amount of product or service. By converting to dollars one can determine what a single item costs. Increase output or decrease input and productivity goes up. Nowhere is the issue of competence, effort, or behavior involved. It is merely *assumed* that output is a function of these things. Such an assumption has never been proved and never will be. The assumption is the great management myth expressed as:

$$\text{Performance} = \text{Skill} \times \text{Effort}$$

If one accepts this seemingly innocent formula, than it is quite natural to emphasize motivational gimmicks to increase effort and training programs to improve skills. Unfortunately, there is a flaw in the equation: we don't know what skill is required to achieve a particular level of performance; we can only guess and make assumptions. Thus, we can determine the "right" way to manage an organization until someone does it "wrong" and succeeds. If that person is the president, we change our assumptions. If the person is a supervisor, we punish that behavior as "wrong."

What we need are means to relate effort and performance that do not rely on such assumptions. To find them, we must take the fundamentals of human behavior and *measurably* relate them to achievement. To begin at the beginning, Rule 1 tells us that people always act in their own best interests; they expend effort the way they spend money, trying to get the most value for the least cost. Value, however, is a perceptual concept: the cost of producing something does not determine what people will pay for it; that is a function of need which is also perceptual. Thus, Rule 2: people act to meet perceived needs. This was best illustrated in England during World War II, when the work week was expanded from 40 to 50 hours in defense plants. Total output did not increase one iota; people just paced themselves differently. On the other hand, some modern plants have reduced working hours and increased total output. That, sports fans, is productivity improvement. Here, then, is a better formula for defining performance.

$$\text{Performance} = \frac{\text{Competence} \times \text{Value}}{\text{Effort}}$$

People will perform better whenever the payoff (value) increases or the effort required diminishes. Competence in this sense is defined by the capacity to achieve results. It differs from skill in that it is a measure of physical limits rather than of trainable abilities. Thus, the real star of any game may be the one who sweats *least* and gets the job done, not the guy who is drenched in perspiration just to keep up.

The Dilemma of Competence

Rule 12 states that when goals are not measurable, form replaces function. Achievement of goals is the primary measure of performance. Thus, when goals are *not* measurable, attention is directed toward competence. But competence is not directly quantifiable.

Indeed, there is no such thing as an incompetent person, only a person not competent to do a particular job. Therefore, competence can be measured by deduction, but only if performance is made measurable. The saving grace is Rule 13: all goals are measurable. The logic goes like this:

1. To evaluate competence, performance must be measurable.
2. For performance to be measured, quantitative goals must be established.
3. To establish quantitative goals, there must be standards of performance.

Devotees of games are quick to establish such standards. The .300 hitter in baseball and the million-dollar insurance salesperson are good examples of high standards. Although somewhat arbitrary, they are based on a historical perspective of what represents "good" performance. It is a standard—and as always that is the key.

Given that a standard is established so that performance becomes measurable, we can define competence with a little algebraic manipulation that yields Rule 25.

$$Rule\ 25:\ \text{Competence} = \frac{\text{Performance} \times \text{Effort}}{\text{Value}}$$

A person's competence is thus measured by the results achieved (performance), the effort expended, and the payoff involved. Skill is defined as a particular level of performance for a given amount of effort. A student with A skills who does B work does not value the task enough to put out the effort required for a top grade. On the other hand, students with B skills are unlikely to earn A's without superhuman effort, as they are functioning to the limits of their current skill. This is the dilemma of competence: without measurable performance we cajole people to work harder when, in fact, such extra effort may not be worth the price to them. With measurable goals we can determine the nature of the problem. Without them we are left with the frustration, inherent in all dilemmas, that there can be no solution.

Managing for Performance

Most managers are aware of Pareto's Law, which states that 20 ✓ percent of what we do accounts for 80 percent of what we achieve. This principle is true for groups (most sales dollars are obtained by a very few salespeople) and for individuals (most of a manager's time is spent on trivia). Thus, paying attention to behavior is most likely to yield data that have little connection to results. There are, however, four strategies for improving performance that do relate to results. They are:

1. provide accurate *performance data* (feedback)
2. increase *competence* (selection)
3. increase *value* of performance (compensation)
4. decrease *effort* required (training)

The first strategy is the simplest and most powerful. Without performance data there is no hope for improvement; these data are not strokes but rather hard, measurable numbers. Often during an organizational diagnosis I learn that such data are available but hidden. Here is one example.

The Punchatrain Paper Packaging Company produces cartons for the beverage industry. A key production job is that of glue-machine operator. Glue machines are complicated pieces of equipment that require considerable skill. Of the 48 operators, 10 were judged to be performing well below standard. Although daily computer printouts provided extensive data, only foremen saw them. Average performance for the group as a whole was 78 percent of standard. Management was ready to demote the 10 poor performers, but it had no assurance that their replacements would do any better. Thus, they agreed to an experiment.

A large "scoreboard" was constructed and attached to the wall adjoining the time clock. It listed each of the crews by name, followed by a box for each work day. At the end of each shift, the foreman wrote in the performance to standard for the crews. The board was erased at the end of each week. Those who averaged 100 percent or better for the week received a gold star next to their name. Thus, feedback was fairly immediate, but each week began with a clean slate.

In the first month, production increased to 83 percent; in the second month, 89 percent; and in the third month it approached 100 percent. More important, 8 of the 10 poor performers were now producing at an acceptable level. All of this was accomplished without changing levels of competence, the effort required, or the monetary value of the job. What was changed was the *psychological* value of the job: the workers were shown that anything worth putting up on a huge scoreboard must be of value. Further, by getting constant feedback, poor performers were able to make a connection between their behavior and results. Finally, those with gold stars who saw that the game was not zero-sum began to coach their peers.

The scoreboard approach is not a panacea. It assumes that people have been selected on the basis of competence, trained to perform well, and provided with an incentive to excel. When these conditions do exist, feedback is often the solution to performance problems. In the following chapters, however, we will explore those situations in which such criteria have not been met and how to deal with them.

References

McGregor, Douglas, "An Uneasy Look at Performance Appraisal." *Harvard Business Review,* May–June, 1957.

Meyer, Herbert H., Emanuel Kay, and John R. P. French, Jr., "Split Roles in Performance Appraisal." *Harvard Business Review,* January–February 1965.

14
Selection

A good man is hard to find.
Famous bounty hunter

George Thompson was the hottest sales rep to hit the New England branch office in a month of Sundays. With a blend of drive and charisma, he spun his magic from Bangor to Bridgeport. A bright, charming man, George rushed in where angels feared to tread. From morning to night, he relentlessly pursued every prospect he could find. In his second year, he made the big time. He was selected as "Salesman of the Year." As a reward, he and his wife were sent to bask in the sun of a Bahama beach.

Meanwhile, George's supervisors were meeting to deal with a much less pleasant task. The Atlanta branch was in deep trouble. Sales were way under quota for two consecutive quarters, and there hadn't been a dime's worth of new business in three. Rumor had it that the office was in constant turmoil. Several salespeople had already quit.

The vice-president of sales stared out the window of his spacious corner office. He felt both anger and frustration. "It is like a juggling act," he thought. "Get a grip on one situation and another pops up." With a sigh, he swung his chair back to face the group. The obvious decision hung like a dark cloud of gloom. Herb Foster, the Atlanta manager, wasn't cutting it. He would have to be replaced. With a vague feeling of *déjà vu*, the VP addressed his staff, "All right, gentlemen, who do we put in Atlanta?"

Enter our well-tanned hero. The word comes down from the corporate obelisk: George is to be promoted. With great fanfare and a roar of moving vans, the Thompsons head South. He is, after all, the obvious choice. "A bit of a hot dog," his manager says, "but he's the best we've got. Hopefully, he'll mature in the position." Hopefully.

Back in Atlanta, Herb is cleaning out his desk. He shakes his head in bewilderment. Just a few short years ago he was riding high. As top sales person in the Dallas branch, he won all the awards. The computer spit out his bonus checks like a slot machine gone beserk. Then came the call to Atlanta—a promotion. He was moving up. "Damn," he now thinks, "I wish I had said no."

Like some ritual dance, this scene recurs hundreds of times each year throughout corporate America. Star performers are moved into supervisory positions in the hope they will take hold and perform. More often than not, the result is a horrendous waste of time, talent, and effort. Yet the cycle goes on as organizations squander valuable human resources they can ill afford to lose. For many organizations, the loss is double: they demoralize competent individuals and fail to meet their needs for talented management.

In this chapter we will take a hard, pragmatic look at the performance of effective and ineffective managers. After reviewing both the facts and the fads of management selection, concrete suggestions will be offered as to how one can reduce the probability of failure.

Competence

People succeed at jobs for the darnedest reasons. This is neither unique to business nor uncommon to organizations in general. From recruitment to retirement, the task of predicting the performance of a complex human being with an unclear role in a constantly changing environment is monumental. While the probability of securing competent performance has remained constant, the stakes for doing so (higher labor costs) have piled up at an incredibly rapid rate. Technology is no longer likely to bail organizations out of the wicked spiral of growing inflation that has combined with marginal productivity improvement. A good place to start is the selection of the managers who must steer their organizations through this economic turmoil. In many cases, they are both the solution and the problem.

Business clings tenaciously to the myth that successful individual performers are the best candidates for managerial positions. At times, quite the opposite is true. Indeed, many of the behaviors that form the basis for the effectiveness of individual contributors are the same ones that cause their poor performance as managers. The sports world is an excellent example of this phenomenon. Note how few consistently successful team managers were themselves superstar athletes.

To return to our story, the similarities between George's and Herb's behavior are striking. Both are ambitious, aggressive men with great charm and a strong need to convince others. They thrive on and seek the immediate feedback of a sales call. Faced with the obligations of a branch manager, they stumble over the behaviors that once served them so well. This is why behavior is so often irrelevant to performance.

To get down to cases, the dilemma of competence is founded on a great deal of misunderstanding about predicting the performance of people on a job. To develop a firm foundation for management selection, three facts need to be established.

Fact 1: Focus on failure, not success.

Success in a job is impossible to predict accurately; in the best of situations, the odds are prohibitive. If you accept that individual performance and managerial performance are independent events like drawing an ace from a deck of cards, then traditional management selection aims to draw aces back to back (for which the odds are more than 200 to 1 against).

What *can* be predicted is failure—specific behaviors that will so impede performance that success is next to impossible. These behaviors *are* relevant. In our story, the vice-president asked the wrong questions. It would have been more productive to ponder, "Why did Herb fail?" Indeed, as in most situations, the fault lies not in the solution but in understanding the problem clearly.

There is a corollary to this issue, which is the need for a manager to understand the technology of his or her business. The fact is granted, but not the necessity that one be a star performer.

> *Fact 2:* Managers fail for nontechnical reasons (Rule 17).

The continued promotion of star performers into supervisors who achieve the most meager results is testimony to this fact. The failure of managers to perform effectively is almost always attributable to nontechnical skill. The ability to achieve excellent results through other people remains independent of technical expertise, be it sales or sandblasting.

> *Fact 3:* Individuals tend to be task- or people-oriented, but not both.

There is a tendency, when speaking of failure, to label people much like damaged goods. The more likely reality is a situation in which a person and job just don't go together. All of us have strengths and weaknesses. It is when we find ourselves forced to function from weakness rather than from strength that the dilemma of competence raises its ugly head.

In assessing individual skills and abilities, one major dimension occurs repeatedly. This is a person's orientation toward tasks or people. In his book *The Gamesman* Michael Maccoby described four profiles of managerial behavior. Yet, two of these categories—the "gamesman" and the "jungle fighter"—share a common attribute: insight into their own and others' behavior. Both are oriented toward people rather than things. In contrast, the "craftsman" exemplifies those whose primary orientation is the task at hand. In the fourth category, the "company man," neither orientation appears to dominate. Rather than being a contradiction, this fact leads one to wonder if such an individual can succeed at either side of the plate.

Taken together, these three facts clearly set the stage for understanding managerial performance. Candidates who are task-oriented and lack the nontechnical skills of managing will fail in supervisory positions. The opposite is not true, however: those who do have these nontechnical skills and are people-oriented may still fail. At best, it's a toss-up. Thus, our goal for improving management selection can never be perfection but only significant improvement by reducing predictable failure.

The Nontechnical Behaviors

The real value of defining and labeling management behavior is that it gives people a common frame of reference. There is no magic in any one particular set of categories because it is performance that really counts. The following has been a useful division of behaviors associated with the process of management:

Planning: the ability to establish a goal and decide how it will be achieved.

Organizing: the ability to make a plan work by grouping and delegating authority.

Directing: the ability to guide and influence subordinates to accomplish a set of activities.

Controlling: the ability to measure results, evaluate them, and correct them as necessary.

Most significant nontechnical behaviors (leadership, motivation, decision making, communication, and so on) can be slotted into these four functions. These functions are most useful, however, in that they often provide key bench marks for predicting management failure. By superimposing them on an organizational hierarchy, we can create a "road map" for failure and perhaps a sounder basis for selection, succession planning, and promotional decisions.

In the sales situation previously discussed, the organization had five major levels of organizational responsibility:

Level	Position	Responsibility
1	sales representative	sell
2	branch sales manager	control
3	district sales manager	direct
4	product manager	organize
5	vice-president	plan

At each level of management, a new and unique set of skills is required in addition to all of those needed at the lower levels. Thus, the vice-president must plan, organize, direct, and control the organization. Figure 15 illustrates how managers can and do fail at each level.

With this model as a road map, we can begin to explore and understand how and why managers fail. Then and only then can we begin to plan strategies for avoiding these performances.

Controlling

When an ace salesman arrives to assume a supervisory role, he is fresh from a whole series of victories as a competent, effective performer in one-on-one situations. Usually he has little insight into why he has been so effective; it just seems to come naturally. Indeed, most of his accomplishments in life have been a result of his great drive and ability to convince others.

But in his new position, the rules have changed. He is hit with a constant barrage of meetings, interpersonal squabbles, and paperwork. Removed from the "action," he attempts to "sell" his subordinates on increasing their performance. He becomes frus-

Figure 15.   **A model for failure.**

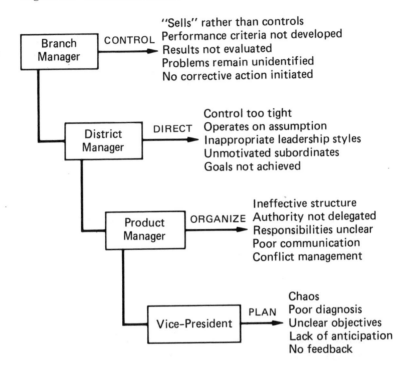

trated when they do not behave as he would. "All I do is wait for something to happen," he complains.

The gleam of the managerial position begins to dull. He realizes too late that he is playing someone else's game. Without the skills to develop performance criteria and evaluate results, problems do not get identified. Dealing with symptoms rather than causes, his days are filled with crises and "firefighting."

The skill in achieving results through others rests on the ability to evaluate performance. The psychological requirement is good insight into one's own and others' behavior. Without such insight, a manager is flying blind and is most likely to crash into unanticipated problems. Some people have an ear for music, others for people.

The greatest barrier to effective management is a "tin ear" toward the wants and needs of others.

Directing

How can an individual be successful at one level of management and yet fail at another? Having jumped over successive hurdles of individual competence and small-group control, one would think only the most able would remain. After all, aren't all management functions about the same? Alas, no. Just as the skills required for a first-line manager differ from those for an individual contributor, so are there different requirements for one who manages managers.

In our last example, branch managers could reach out and touch the people who were directly responsible for sales results. The district manager, however, had no such direct control. Some managers at this level, in an attempt to retain the "feel" of their former position, pull too tightly on the reins. Rather than greater direction, the result is often an organization that rears up and drops the manager on his or her head.

At this level, mere sensitivity to people is insufficient. The manager must be able to assess each situation and alter his or her own behavior. That is, in addition to having a good ear, the manager must also be able to pluck the right strings. As Fred Fiedler points out in his book on leadership, the effectiveness of a particular style is contingent upon leader-subordinate relations, task structure, and power position. Failure to choose the appropriate style often results in subordinates who feel little motivation and, ultimately, goals that are not achieved.

Organizing

A great deal of conceptual clarity was added to understanding organizational functioning by the theory of differentiation and integration, developed by Paul Lawrence and Jay Lorsch. Put simply, this theory states that an organization with different functional departments has managers who differ in their cognitive and emotional orientations (differentiation). But it requires collaboration to achieve unity of effort (integration). Thus, the battle lines are drawn for interdepartmental conflicts.

Into this breach is thrust the third-level manager, who must supervise people whose area of technical expertise is different from his or her own and each other's. The critical skill required here is an ability to resolve conflict. The conceptual goal is to achieve integration in an organization that is experiencing differentiation. The strategy requires considerations of structure, authority, responsibility, and communication.

In our sales example, it is the product manager on whom this burden falls. This time a "good ear" and nimble direction are not enough; this manager must be able to *orchestrate* sales, marketing, and other diverse functions reporting to him or her. The result can be a symphony of productivity or a cacophony of conflict.

Planning

To survive, it is crucial that an organization know what business it is in and to act on that knowledge (the corollary of Rule 10). Planning in its simplest form is knowing where you are, where you are going, and how you will get there. It is also helpful if barriers (problems) can be anticipated and feedback provided for.

The most significant aspect of the planning process is the rare and unique ability to achieve perspective—that is, to step back and see the forest as well as the trees. No wonder those who have it are often described as people with "vision," and those who don't find themselves and their organizations arriving too late with too little.

The Tools of Selection: Fads and Facts

Basically there are five techniques available for the selection of management talent. The following table itemizes these tools in order of their relative cost, risk, and payoff in terms of predicting success or failure on the job. Cost in this case represents the time, effort, and money needed to develop the tool. Risk involves the price paid for wrong decisions. Payoff is a subjective estimate of the current value of each. The techniques are summarized in the accompanying table.

The Tools of Selection

Tool	Cost	Risk	Payoff	
			Success	Failure
Job Trial	Low	High	Low	High
Simulation	High	Low	Low	High
Interview	Low	Low	Low	Moderate
Tests	Low	Low	Low	Low
Personal History	Low	Low	Low	Low

Job Trial

In spite of the high risk involved, job trial continues to be the technique of manager selection that is most relied upon. In our story, first Herb and then George are thrust into management jobs to sink or swim on their own; job trial is indeed the most accurate method for predicting failure. But at what a high cost. While there is nothing inherently immoral about this trial-and-error approach, it is criminal that so little attention is paid to those who do not succeed. Because of the "up or out" policy operating in our example, competent individuals may well be taking their talent and experience elsewhere. Alas, in fact, many companies have the reputation for being marvelous training grounds for their competitors.

It is more usual, however, for managers to rise to their level of incompetence, *à la* the "Peter Principle," and stay there. The negative payoff here can be devastating in terms of poor management and thwarted potential.

Simulation

In order for most pilots and all astronauts to prove their competence, they must pass rigorous exercises in a "simulator"; no one is willing to take the downside risk of poor choice. Indeed, the job of pilot is an excellent example of failure-focused selection. Pilots are paid excessively for taking off, pointing out the Grand Canyon, and landing. But what they are really paid for are the rare emergencies when, as far as the passengers are concerned, they earn their lifetime salary in one flight. Once again, Pareto's Law holds true (20 percent of what you do accounts for 80 percent of your results).

For the manager, too, it is the crises, the key decisions, the rare blaze of innovation that truly reflects his or her impact. And therein lies the reason why it is impossible to predict success. To generate critical behaviors, there must be a sense of reality—that is, the opportunity to fail. Job trials provide this reality; so do well-designed simulations.

In recent years, the emergence of the assessment center as a management tool has demonstrated the effectiveness of simulation. As an alternative to job trial, simulation can produce behaviors associated with planning, organizing, directing, and controlling without the accompanying risks of failure on the job. The trade-off, however, is the expense involved to develop such a program, particularly when there are few candidates and fewer future openings.

The Interview

An interview is the third-best way to select a manager. It is also the most widely used. When it is failure-focused and zeroes in on critical dimensions, it can begin to approximate the payoffs of job trial and simulation. Too often, however, it is an exercise in futility.

Interviewing is an unnatural act. We are taught as children that if you can't say something good about a person, you should say nothing. Yet, the power of an interview is in the opportunity to generate and evaluate critical behaviors associated with negative performance. Thus, the development of effective interviewing skills involves as much the *unlearning* of old habits as it does the acquisition of new knowledge. But most interviewers have not had a day's worth of training. Their performance shows it. Here are some tips from the pros:

— Have a list of knock-out factors (remember you are looking to predict failure, not success).
— Have a plan to ensure full coverage.
— Take notes (so you can go back and probe potential negatives).
— Pair up (two interviewers are much less likely to miss key data).
— Beware of the "halo effect" (the tendency for brillance in one area to blind you to limitations in another).

As a way to reinforce failure-focused interviews, interviewers should be prepared to answer two key questions. First, if this candidate is hired and fails, what behavior will have caused it? Second, what is your estimate of the probability that he or she will fail? All management selection involves risk. The best we can do is be clear about the odds. Don't avoid long shots; just be sure the payoff is equally long.

Tests

The best employment test ever developed is the typing test. For a job that requires constant use of a typewriter, it is a perfect example of simulation. No standardized paper-and-pencil test has yet been devised to simulate the job of a manager, but this is not to say it can't be done. The key word is *standardized*. To be effective, such a test must focus on the specific behaviors that cause failure in an organization. "Off the rack" stuff just won't fit. As for the plethora of quickie multiple-choice packages of management tests on the market, who is kidding whom?

A glimmer of hope in this area has been the increasing use of an individually administered assessment-center exercise in selection situations. The "in-basket exercise," when custom-designed for an organization, can be a very effective tool. (In the exercise, the candidate is given a case problem via a stack of correspondence and must sort through it to build a plan of action.) Note, however, that such an exercise is not *scored* in the traditional sense; rather, it forms the basis for an in-depth interview. Thus, its effectiveness is highly dependent on the skill of the interviewer, and the exercise will not compensate for an interviewer who lacks the appropriate skills.

Personal History

How people have behaved in past situations is often predictive of how they will react to similar situations in the future. We know, for example, that a man with a great number of financial obligations is much less likely to quit a job impulsively than one who is independently wealthy. We also know that if he has a history of long tenure in jobs, he is less likely to "job hop." These and related "facts" have encouraged some organizations to develop personal-history questionnaires to identify such behaviors. But because these devices rest on the notion of "similar situations," their long-term utility is suspect, particularly when the criterion for success is something other than tenure.

When tenure *is* the target, however, there are certain situations in which this questionnaire can be a valuable addition to the management-selection process. A prime example is a job that will involve living in a foreign country. Regardless of their management skill, some people just cannot cope with culture shock. We have found this particularly true of assignments in underdeveloped countries, where the shock can be profound.

Recommendations

The task of selecting competent managers is not an easy one. And it is not made any easier by trying to focus on what can't be predicted. Failure-focused approaches are based on the notion that while you can't win them all, you can lose less often.

I used a sales organization as an example because results tend to be visibly measurable and reaction to poor performance swift. But the same dilemma exists for other lines of progression: chief operator to foreman, accountant to controller, plant manager to division manager, and so on. In each case, top performers are shunted into management jobs for all the wrong reasons. So how do we resolve this dilemma?

Let's return to our sales story one last time. Let's assume that the company does a pretty good job of selecting sales representatives. Indeed, even if their strategy is nothing more than a job trial, it involves relatively small risks compared with those inherent in hiring for higher-level jobs. Selection for these higher levels might be performed as follows.

Branch Sales Managers

A BSM assessment center is designed to identify those control skills that are critical to the job. Since there are a large number of BSM positions in the company, this approach is deemed cost effective. Participants are selected on the basis of their meeting *minimum* proficiency standards on their current job. Those who are identified as high risk (likely to fail) for the position of branch sales manager are counseled to meet their career needs through selling rather than managing. No stigma is attached to this course of action.

District Sales Managers

Branch sales managers who have met the minimum requirements of their job are interviewed by teams of higher-level managers who are encouraged to focus on the candidates' directing skills. Included in these is discussion and evaluation of performance on a DSM in-basket exercise. High-risk candidates are told they may be moved to larger branches but are not candidates for the next level up.

Product Managers

At this level the air becomes greatly rarefied. Candidates are few, and potential opportunities fewer still. Top management must develop great skill to interview with an eye toward candidates' organizing skills. Many individuals can direct and control subordinates who share their own area of technical expertise. But when they can no longer *personally* evaluate each performer, many slip and fall. Current product managers are encouraged to give their subordinates projects that require organizing skills and to evaluate the performance of each.

To compensate for possible lack of evaluative skill among top managers, an independent professional—in this case, a staff psychologist familiar with the organization—could be included on the interviewing schedule.

Vice-Presidents

If management is an art, at this level we must separate the masters from the journeymen; it requires great insight to identify the absence of truly effective planning skills. Fortunately, the job of product manager can provide many opportunities to demonstrate these skills. The key for the selection committee is to factor them out of the day-to-day stuff.

Here, too, a professional third party can be extremely useful, not so much to lend interviewing expertise as to add perspective and clarity to what is already there. In our story, the VP laments about the juggling act he must perform. Elsewhere in that meeting was a man who not only juggled better but enjoyed it as well.

Outside Candidates

The preceding strategies are based on the assumption of promotion from within. At times, however, these procedures will lead to the unpleasant revelation that all inside candidates are high risks. Too often this knowledge results in either a resolute sigh of "he's the best we've got" or a mad dash to call the nearest headhunter.

In the former case, the company is betting its future on long shots. And in the latter, it may base its decision on insufficient data, which is not an argument against outside candidates, but a reminder that their record was achieved on a different track. Thus, each of the requisite behaviors must be explored in depth; nothing can be assumed.

If the cupboard is bare at higher levels of management, the company can and should take short- and long-term remedial actions that involve the infusion of fresh outside talent. On the other hand, if this dilemma is faced at the lowest level, there are perhaps more serious problems. Either the organization is not attracting those with management potential, or it doesn't know how to find them from within.

References

Byham, William C., "Assessment Centers for Spotting Future Managers." *Harvard Business Review*, July–August 1970.

Fiedler, Fred E., *A Theory of Leadership Effectiveness*. New York: McGraw-Hill, 1967.

Lawrence, Paul R., and Jay W. Lorsch, *Organization & Environment*. Homewood, Ill.: Richard D. Irwin, 1969.

Maccoby, Michael, *The Gamesman*. New York: Simon & Schuster, 1976.

Peter, Lawrence J., and Raymond Hull, *The Peter Principle*. New York: Morrow, 1969.

15

Compensation

All that glitters is not gold.

Famous alchemist

In a court of law one receives "compensation" for pain or injury. That such a word is used to describe the relationship between money and work is further evidence that the myth that punishment changes behavior continues. Any wonder then that many managers use the threat of withholding economic rewards as a prime means of exercising authority? They see money as a reward for effort that is punishing. The individual is perceived as giving up control in exchange for cash benefits.

There is certainly a great deal of truth in the notion that money and performance are related. However, no direct cause-and-effect relationship has ever been established between the two, the reason being that the true value of compensation is a function of the particular need being met. Consider that the same amount of compensation will have a different impact for:

1. A person who is deeply in debt.
2. A person who is independently wealthy.
3. A person with a large family.
4. A person who is single.
5. A person who is making more than his or her peers.
6. A person who is making less than his or her peers.
7. A person who has performed well.
8. A person who has performed poorly.

Organizations, in an effort to meet their needs for profit, by definition want to pay the least amount of compensation in return for an acceptable level of output. To pay more would be wasteful; to pay less would increase the likelihood that performance would drop due to turnover and the related costs of hiring and training new employees. The major difficulty is establishing the worth of a job, for both the organization and the individual. Consider, too, that compensation covers a broad range of items; it is not just a paycheck.

While productivity can be clearly defined in most cases by equating income with labor cost, no such precision exists for the relationship between effort and compensation. It is not true that people will work harder or more intelligently for more money. Rather, the *perceived value* of compensation has an effect on overall performance. While this effect cannot be precisely defined, it does raise the question of how well people's needs are being explored, defined, and met in terms of their compensation.

An example of this kind of approach would be to arrive at a total dollar figure for compensating a particular job but to give the individual *choices* about how that money would be distributed across such categories as pay, benefits, vacation time, and so on. In a sense, this is an extension of the flex-time approach—call it "flex-pay," if you like, or the "cafeteria" approach, as some companies have called it. The point is that just as people's work-hour needs differ, so do their needs with respect to compensation. The overall objective is to meet these needs as effectively as possible in order to generate the most productive use of their talents.

Content

Two issues determine the specific aspects of how organizations administer wages and salaries. First, there is the notion of *equity*—whether the money paid is seen to be fair relative to the job market, the economy, job status, and the effort involved. Second, there is the concept of *incentive*—not the myth that more money will result in more effort, but a response that satisfies a motive, as we discussed earlier.

What, then, *is* the relationship between pay and performance? First, when people perceive a direct connection, they are motivated to perform well. Second, when they do not trust management, they will see any incentive plan as a crooked game. Thus, in order to avoid expending more effort for the same money, people will develop a set of norms against higher performance and punish those who violate it. Pay systems have a major impact on the social systems that develop in work groups. Money significantly influences individual behavior such that people will change in ways that, according to their perceptions, will result in the rewards they prefer. This is just another example of Rule 1 in action (people always act in their own best interest . . .). The key to this issue rests in people's beliefs and perceptions; the failure of most incentive plans is caused by their inability to convince participants that the game is legitimate.

Studies have shown that high absenteeism and turnover can be linked directly to low pay satisfaction. High pay satisfaction has been shown to occur when people believe and trust that they are fairly compensated in relation to others who do the same kind of work.

Such research has also led to a frustrating search for some ideal pay plan that will resolve the dilemma of monetary dissatisfaction, counterproductive behavior, and the disbelief that pay and performance are related. To date, the search has been fruitless, one reason being that changing the mechanics of a pay system deals with content while the problem is one of process. Because we are dealing with beliefs and perceptions, focus should be on how pay decisions are made, including the choice of system. Furthermore, consideration must be given to the fit of such pay decisions to the organizational culture.

Process

The way money is distributed in an organization will largely determine people's perception of pay. In most groups where secrecy is the norm, managers often believe they are paid much less than others at their level. Organizations that do not have this problem appear to have one thing in common: their pay plan was designed and developed by the participants. The fact that more organizations don't experiment with such approaches is testimony to the power of bureaucrats who profess to be experts in wage-and-salary administration as well as to organizations' continuing fascination with logic. The bottom line is that participation will significantly influence the effectiveness of compensation systems—not because the result is any more technically sound, but because participation creates feelings of control over and commitment to what is decided.

For an incentive plan to work, people must see a relationship between pay and performance. Such a perception is based initially on the individuals' trust that what was promised would indeed be delivered. When people participate in designing and administering the plan, they are much more likely to trust it—first, because they have much more information about it, and second, because they perceive a sense of control. In other words, they see themselves as having the power to correct inequities.

Motivation and Organizations

The way in which an organization deals with pay tends to be a very clear indication of its culture. Money is often at the heart of closely held beliefs about people and motivation. Four distinct categories were identified by Roger Harrison:

1. power orientation
2. role orientation
3. task orientation
4. person orientation

A power-oriented organization is characterized by its attempts to dominate others both inside and outside its boundaries (on and off the job). Competition and win-lose struggles prevail, so that pay decisions are often the result of negotiation.

A role-oriented organization is greatly concerned with rules and regulations. Conflict is sublimated by contracts and agreements. Pay and benefits are minutely defined. Harrison distinguishes power and role orientations by comparing them to a dictatorship and a constitutional monarchy, the latter often being a bureaucracy of the first order. A personal experience may serve to further illustrate this.

In 1965 I was offered summer employment by the Department of the Army. My salary would be determined by my grade level. To establish my grade level, I was required to complete a Form 57, which when unfolded was longer than I am, printed on both sides, with very fine print. After due deliberation, I was informed that my background and experience warranted a GS-7 rating. It was a good job that offered the opportunity to learn a great deal about a field I was interested in.

Prior to making my decision, I was contacted by the Department of the Navy, which was also interested in hiring me for the summer. I sent them a copy of my Form 57 and was astounded to learn that they rated me a GS-11, which represented a difference of more than $100 per week. Although the money was tempting, the job itself was not nearly as attractive. I decided to negotiate with the army.

When I reached the Director, I told him of my dilemma and suggested that he split the difference by rating me a GS-9. He told me that it would be against the rules and that the original rating had to stand. I explained that, as an impoverished graduate student, I couldn't afford to give up so much money. His reply still echoes in my mind, "Well, we lose a lot of people to the navy."

In stark contrast, an organization that is task-oriented focuses on the achievement of a superordinate goal. Nothing is allowed to get in the way of accomplishing the task, not even the rules. Indeed, there is little hesitation to break a rule if task accomplishment is furthered by doing so. Such is the nature of small entrepreneurial organizations and those that deal with fast-changing, complex technology. Pay is seen as a means to an end. You pay what is needed to get the job done.

Person-oriented organizations better fit the definition of groups than that of organizations. They exist primarily to serve the needs of their members and, as such, income may not be a primary consideration. Rather, a "reasonable living" for all may be its approach to economic rewards, with the major focus on the work itself. An example of such an orientation would be a small group of professionals who have joined together for research and development.

Individuals and Rewards

In our culture we accept that rewards will be distributed unequally to members of an organization. The effect of those rewards on an individual depends on the intensity of the need met by money, the certainty of the reward (trust), and the cost involved (effort).

Money provides the greatest incentive when the individual's needs are those of survival, located at the bottom of Maslow's hierarchy (see Figure 1). This has been called by some the *discomfort zone*, where there is little or no opportunity for discretionary spending because everything goes for food and shelter.

At the other extreme, the need for self-actualization also has significant impact on monetary rewards. If you offer a person who has a high need for achievement a larger reward, he or she will not perform any better; indeed, the money may distract him or her from the task. However, there is evidence that people with a low need for achievement will exert more effort for more money. Since the task itself offers no intrinsic reward, the money tends to have greater worth.

The relative value of financial increases also plays a significant role in the motivating power of money. That is, a wage or salary increase has to offer the opportunity to change one's basic life style before it can provide a real incentive to increase performance.

All people make judgments about what they receive as compensation for their contribution to an organization's efforts and conclude that it is either fair or unfair. When inequity is perceived in *either* direction, the person will conclude the game is crooked. Thus, even overpayment can restrict output because people do not see any connection between pay and performance.

The power of participative approaches is that individuals can act to reduce perceived inequity. Indeed, without such an approach individuals will take matters into their own hands to deal with unfairness. People will deal with perceived inequity in a number of ways. If they feel underpaid, they may limit their output. The opposite is not often true, although there is evidence that perceived overpayment may result in lower quantity produced *but* at a higher quality.

Another way people deal with pay inequity is to distort the value of their contribution to balance it with the value they place on their compensation. Another common reaction to this situation is escape—either physically by leaving the organization or mentally by going into "neutral" and becoming just a warm body.

Individual Motivation and Organizational Orientation

In a very pragmatic sense, the issue of compensation is the source of much conflict in organizations. Given that the profit motive is seen as the name of the game, it follows that individuals will be perceived as logical game players who are "motivated" to maximize their rewards and minimize their effort. Thus, a zero-sum game of the highest order is established.

The real source of conflict, however, is the lack of fit between the individual's and the organization's needs. By comparing the pyramid of motivation in Chapter 1 (see Figure 1) with Harrison's four organizational character types we can create a matrix of fit and misfit with respect to compensation, as illustrated in the accompanying table.

Four Organizational Character Types

Type	Level of Motivation			
	Achievement	Power	Affiliation	Survival
Task Oriented	FIT	Technocracy	Sweatshop	Perfectionism
Power Oriented	Politics	FIT	Pressure cooker	Dictatorship
Person Oriented	Country Club	Welfare state	FIT	Nepotism
Role Oriented	Red tape	Over regulation	Bureaucracy	FIT

People with a high need for achievement are most comfortable in an organization that is task oriented. They are least comfortable in a power-oriented organization, where frustration results from the perception that there is too much politics going on. A person-oriented organization is also a poor fit, as a "country club" atmosphere seems to exist rather than one that focuses on the work to be done. And there is much complaining about red tape when such people find themselves in a role-oriented organization.

Quite obviously, people with high needs for power fit best in an organization that is so oriented. In task-oriented organizations they perceive themselves surrounded by technocrats who can't see the big picture. Equally frustrating for such people is a role-oriented organization, which they perceive as an overregulated one that prevents competition and free exterprise. And at the other extreme, the person-oriented organization is seen by power-hungry folks as a welfare state in which rewards are often distributed on the basis of need.

A person-oriented organization fits quite nicely, however, for people who have a high need for affiliation. Such people tend to find power-oriented organizations to be pressure cookers in which there is constant jostling for position. Equally uncomfortable for them is the task-oriented operation, where the pressure is also great but work related. They may perceive such a situation as a "sweatshop" in which there is all work and no play. They also have problems with role-oriented organizations, where their affiliative needs may be blocked by the rules, laws, and customs of a bureaucracy.

In contrast, a role-oriented bureaucracy provides a good match for those whose needs are to survive and achieve some level of security. People with such needs find a power-oriented organization to be a dictatorship where the risk of job loss is great. Indeed, any orientation that threatens their survival is found to be unacceptable. They complain of nepotism and influence peddling in person-oriented organizations and of excessive nitpicking and perfectionism in those that are task oriented.

To summarize our discussion of individual motivation and organizational orientation, the fundamental dynamics of money and motivation still stand. The relationship between them is obscure, with far greater opportunity for dissatisfaction than for performance improvement. The silver lining is that managers have considerable latitude to improve the situation, if they can see what is going on.

First and foremost, managers must know what orientation the organization represents. Second, they must assess the level of needs that their subordinates possess. If there is a bad fit between needs and compensation, the problem cannot be solved by any specific pay plan. Rather, attention should be directed at changing the perceptions of one or both sides. If, on the other hand, there is reasonable congruence between the two, the manager should ask three questions:

1. Do people perceive a relationship between pay and performance?
2. Is this relationship seen to be equitable?
3. What is the level of trust?

The answers can provide the source for much conflict resolution and greater productivity.

Finally, there is considerable evidence that open, participative approaches to compensation have a far more effective impact on performance than those that are installed and maintained by edict. Once a person exceeds his level of discomfort, issues of trust and equity become much more critical in establishing money as an incentive for performance.

Most incentive systems do not take these issues into consideration and soon die an ugly death. An exception is a system instituted by one company in the automotive products field that has a reputation for creativity and innovation. Prior to the installation of its incentive program, it gave all employees a 10-percent increase. By betting on the outcome, it swept aside the possibility of mistrust in one fell swoop. The results in terms of productivity improvement were nothing less than spectacular.

A Concluding Note

Most compensation programs are in direct opposition to everything we know about people, groups, and organizations. To change the situation would require a whole restructuring of how pay is perceived and distributed.

To begin with, the whole notion of merit increases is pure nonsense. First, there is rarely a basis for performance distinctions. Second, the difference between a small increase and a large one tends to be minuscule. Indeed, most managers studiously avoid making such distinctions and apportion raises on a relatively flat distribution. Third, the process is so mechanized that one cannot see any direct relationship to effort or results. Fourth, such increases tend to be expected, so that their impact is only significant if they *don't* materialize. And fifth, once a person receives an increase, it becomes part of salary and is paid out for the rest of his or her service, regardless of changes in performance.

A better plan would be to provide all employees with a cost-of-living increase tied to the rate of inflation, which is what merit increases tend to be anyway. (And those who don't get them or receive something less than they expected feel punished and may "act out" their disappointment in counterproductive ways.) In essence, such an approach would promise the same pay for the same work by maintaining the purchasing power of each dollar earned.

Part and parcel of such a program would be a bonus system that is tied directly to performance, with responsibility for distribution delegated downward in the organization. Thus, the president would, in a good year, distribute a lump sum to each vice-president based on that department's performance. The vice-president would assign bonuses to his or her direct subordinates based on their individual performance. The vice-president, however, would not be part of that distribution, as the president would determine his or her bonus. In similar fashion, each of the vice-presidents' subordinates would distribute a lump sum to *their* subordinates, and so on down to the lowest level of supervision.

The power of such an approach is twofold. First, it puts pressure on managers to assess results and thus sharpen the relationship between pay and performance. Second, each year is a "clean slate." With no expectation of automatically awarded bonuses, there is pressure to establish and achieve specific measurable goals that represent a state of equity.

Since this is a book about reality, it must be pointed out that most organizations would resist such an approach. Those that are power-oriented would dislike letting go of the purse strings. Those that are role-oriented would find great discomfort in its lack of structure. Person-oriented organizations would greatly fear for the needy, and the task-oriented outfit would see the whole process as irrelevant to getting the work done.

Reference

Harrison, Roger, "Understanding Your Organization's Character." *Harvard Business Review*, May–June 1972.

16

Training

Let that be a lesson to you.

Famous teacher

Like so many things in the world, the process of learning is neither difficult nor complex until we begin to embroider what we know with what we think we know. Simply defined, learning is a process whereby a person modifies his or her behavior in order to achieve a result that was not possible before. It is the pure acquisition of a skill that the person did not have prior to the process. The result of learning is that the skill is developed. If the skill isn't developed, then learning did not take place. It is a straightforward go–no-go proposition. Reading a book or riding a bike are but two examples. All learning involves five concrete steps:

1. a perceived need
2. training (acquisition of skill)
3. practice
4. feedback
5. reinforcement

Training is only one part of the learning process. But it often gets the most attention, because "education" is a social construct that attempts to create learning but can only control one-fifth of the action. Even then it attempts to take a simple yes/no dichotomy and weave a whole tapestry of measurable responses. Pedagogues have added a new twist to Rule 12: not only does form replace function in the absence of measurable goals, but they then measure the hell out of the form. Unable to deal with the trauma of pass/fail, we inflict learners with a plethora of letters, numbers, and plus and minus signs. The answer to the question of why Johnny can't read is quite simple: he didn't learn how. Everything else that has been written on the subject is a dialogue of guilt and blame by people who may or may not be responsible. In a recent court case, a mother sued a school system when she "discovered" that her 17-year-old daughter had been graduated from high school without being able to read. One can only imagine the home environment that would enable such a situation to go undetected for so long. On the other hand, it is relatively easy to visualize an educational bureaucracy that can't or won't insist that literacy be a requisite for completion.

The Need to Learn

As with all needs, the need to acquire a particular skill is more perceptual than pragmatic. Once again the dilemma of competence, in which behavior and performance become confused, rears its ugly head. Thus, although I never mastered the art of tying my own shoelaces, I get by quite nicely by wearing loafers and slip-ons. In sharp contrast, I can, after more than two decades, still parallel park a '57 Chevy with great ease. It is only when we place *value* on such tasks that this dilemma becomes a problem. And value is pure perception, with or without the numbers. What we have is another case of the solution being part of the problem. That is, while learning is a crisply defined occurrence, training is not.

Consider the most elemental of all behavior modification—toilet training. Experienced parents know that if the need is not present, their efforts will be wasted. Conversely, having the skill is not enough to keep baby dry. Only when both need and ability exist will practice, feedback, and reinforcement pay off. Indeed, as with most training, the separate skills are already present; it is the particular *combination* of those skills plus the *connection* of cause and effect that produces mastery. The same is true for higher-level functions. The ability to recognize shapes and sounds is not literacy, but it is a prerequisite. The skill of connecting meaning to written words is what we define as reading. Such a skill is of little use in training if a person does not place value on the outcome. To tie this all together, we must distinguish between skill and ability. Skill is behavior that is learned. Ability is behavior that is possessed. When a baby has the ability to control the appropriate muscle groups, it then may learn the skill of hitting the socially approved target. Likewise, if a person lacks the ability to distinguish letters and words, the opportunity to learn the skill of reading does not exist. The following rule summarizes the issue of need:

$$\text{Rule 26: Need to learn} = \frac{\text{Value of the skill}}{\text{Cost to acquire}}$$

Establishing the need to learn, if such a need does not already exist, requires that the skill be perceived as having great value in relation to the cost of acquiring it. Since programs designed to promote the notion that "reading is fun" are presented by the same folks who push the idea that school is fun, there is a real credibility gap for kids who do not get support for its value from any other source. All the tools in the world won't teach reading or leading if the need is not there. To create that need is the real challenge of education.

Training

Learning is the process of acquiring a skill, and it is a function of need and ability. This is represented by Rule 27.

$$\text{Rule 27: Learning a skill} = \text{Ability} \times \text{Need}$$

A person who has a great deal of ability does not require much incentive to learn new skills because the cost is relatively low. Conversely, when an individual does not have much ability in an area, he or she requires a strong need to overcome the deficiency and cause learning to occur. In other words, there must be considerable value placed on the skill to be learned.

However simplistic this sounds, it is at the core of what is wrong with most training. It is particularly critical in organizations because they lack the leverage of public schools, which at least have the opportunity to create needs through the value of grades and graduation. And they have tremendous control in terms of structuring content and process. Business and industry, however, tend to treat training in such narrow ways that needs are rarely considered a great deal.

A way out of this bind has been the increasing use of *learning contracts,* in which the learner must be very explicit about what he or she is to accomplish. When adults decide they want to learn something (a perceived need), they tend to think in terms of a project rather than a package of skills—for example, developing a department budget rather than acquiring greater accounting knowledge. The focus is on performance, not behavior. Indeed, the mere process in which teacher and student discuss what has to be learned is a powerful step forward.

Practice

The old saw that "practice makes perfect" contains more than a grain of truth; learning is a process of successive approximation in which mastery is achieved through making and correcting mistakes. Error is a vital ingredient in this process. Given average ability, one learns to ride a bike partly by falling off. This is clearly illustrated by the *learning curve,* shown in Figure 16.

Ability is the base line upon which skill is developed. Although there is considerable variation among individuals, it is particularly significant that for most tasks people already possess most, if not all, of the skills required. The difference between mediocrity and mastery is most often practice—that is, the opportunity to make mis-

Figure 16. **The learning curve.**

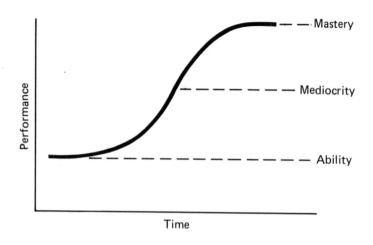

takes and correct them. Without such opportunity, a person's learning curve flattens out, and performance remains mediocre.

A case in point occurred at the Black Box Company. A box machine is run by a crew of three: operator, stacker, and packer. The machine takes sheets of corrugated "board" and folds and glues them into a box. The operator is responsible for keeping the machine running to standard in terms of quantity and quality. The stacker loads corrugated board at one end, and the packer unloads the finished product at the other and bales the boxes for shipment.

In recent years the average crew's performance had been steadily declining, and management was divided on the cause. Some managers argued that the newer operators lacked the mechanical ability to run the machines and pointed to the fact that, as a group, the younger crews performed well below the old-timers. Others felt that more training was the answer, pointing to the fact that through expansion of personnel and machines it took much less time to move up the line of progression (stacker to packer to operator) than it did previously. The first group of managers disagreed, citing the very elegant training program that had been developed complete with diagrams, slides, and videotaped instruction.

In actual fact, both groups were right about the symptoms but wrong about the problem. First, the job title of operator was a misnomer. Everyone on the crew knew how to start the machine and turn it off. The critical skill was troubleshooting. The major barriers to operating at standard were jams and breakdowns, and effective operators knew how to get the machine "back on the line" quickly and efficiently. Poorer operators, however, stood around and waited for help. The training program taught operators how to operate the machine, but not how to fix it.

In the past, operators had learned troubleshooting through a long apprenticeship of stacking and packing. Each time the machine went down, they would observe what went wrong and what action the operator took. Over time they began to recognize the most common problems and their solutions. Indeed, some of the old-timers took great pleasure in letting junior crew members "try their hand." Also, since these operators tended to have many years of service and were entitled to several weeks of vacation, the stackers and packers frequently moved up for that time and thus practiced their newly learned skills further.

This was not the case in recent years, however. While in the past it took ten years to reach the operator level, now it only took ten months. Combined with increasing retirements among operators, the result was a number of "green" crews who had neither learned the necessary skills nor had the opportunity to develop them through trial and error. And since management was unwilling to allow mistakes, operators were often shunted aside during a breakdown so that someone else could fix the machine. The net result was a group of operators who had flattened out on the learning curve and could not troubleshoot.

The solution was twofold. First, the top operators were identified and given a significant role in the process. They were asked to identify the most common problems and the actions required. An off-hours troubleshooting course was developed based on the data they provided. The course consisted of preprogrammed breakdowns on actual machines, for which the student was required to find and implement corrective action. Second, the top operators were encouraged to let their less skilled peers attempt to troubleshoot their machines on the job before jumping in themselves. In ten weeks almost all of the poor performers had raised their output above the standard. The cost saving to the company far exceeded the expenses involved in creating the course. And the company avoided the significant loss of production that might have occurred if operators had been allowed to practice on the machines during working hours.

To sum up, learning takes place over a period of time. It begins at a particular level of ability and is evidenced by a sharp increase in performance. When the learner is allowed to correct his or her own errors, there is a good chance that the skill will be mastered. Otherwise, however, performance will level off prematurely and result in mediocrity. In the words of my tennis pro: if you only play once a week, the best you can hope for is that your skills won't deteriorate.

Feedback

In a previous chapter we described a case in which the construction of a scoreboard significantly improved the performance of machine operators. As we saw, a major cause of performance problems is simply the lack of accurate, timely feedback. Without feedback people have no way to distinguish between correct and incorrect responses. Thus, practice becomes an exercise in futility. For example, when a professor was recently turned down for a promotion, he argued that his twenty years of experience demanded it. The dean's response was that he had only one year's experience repeated twenty times.

Almost all occupations suffer from this kind of stagnation, from farmers who think crop rotation is a passing fad to surgeons who continue to yank out tonsils like weeds in a berry patch. It is still the factory, however, that has the greatest opportunity to improve performance through feedback. Consider this story.

Henry Wilkerson was a young anthropologist who became fascinated with factory work. Swapping his tweeds for overalls he joined the blue-collar ranks and observed a strange paradox. For eight hours a day he and his peers were paid a substantial wage to push buttons and pull levers. There was little apparent satisfaction in these tasks, and much time was devoted to fussing about coffee breaks, grieving about injustices, and fighting over who got the soft jobs.

Yet, after work these same people headed straight for a nearby tavern to pump quarters into a pinball machine. Ironically, they were now *paying* money to push buttons and pull levers. And what was the reward for doing well? They got to do it all over again! Being a good scientist, Henry asked himself what was different. His answer was bells, buzzers, and flashing lights—feedback. Plants, too, have bells and buzzers, but they only go off when something is wrong. When performance is good, nothing happens.

I had occasion to apply Henry's discovery to one of my own clients. The Pro-Products Company manufactured, among other things, small propane tanks for camp stoves, lanterns, and torches. The manufacturing process involved stamping out two-piece shells from sheet metal, welding them together, welding a valve at one end, water testing them for leaks, spray painting them, filling the tanks with gas, and packing them in a box—all for an item that sold for 99 cents in discount stores. Just to break even, the plant had to manufacture 30,000 units in one day. Sometimes they did and sometimes they didn't. On the average, they were slightly below their break-even point.

An interesting feature of the plant was a powerful public-address system. Its use appeared to be restricted to paging managers and workers in the plant. Performance feedback was provided on a bulletin board for the previous week.

In meeting with the various managers, I learned two critical pieces of information. First, supervisors tracked production closely and thus knew the output on an hourly basis. Second, the goal was to manufacture 10 percent over break-even, or 33,000 tanks.

As an experiment, management agreed to try the following program:

1. Employees were told of the 33,000-unit goal.
2. This was translated into an hourly goal of 4,125 units (33,000 ÷ 8 hours).
3. Every hour the number of tanks packed was announced the PA system.
4. When the hourly number met or exceeded the goal, a tape of people cheering was played.
5. At the end of the day, the total production figure was announced over the PA system.
6. When this met or exceeded the goal, a taped victory march was played.

The result was spectacular. The plant soon began to produce tanks at well above the established goal. This created a new challenge—how to maintain that level of performance over the long haul—which is the subject of the next section.

Reinforcement

A critical issue in learning is whether a newly acquired skill will become a permanent part of an individual's repertoire. Merely learning to perform a task is rarely a sufficient reward in itself, particularly if it flows from the needs of others rather than those of the learner, as in the above case.

The major objective here is how to maintain changes in behavior. Losing weight or quitting smoking is not difficult to do; the hard part is staying off sweets or cigarettes. Skill training is *not* the answer. Indeed, most dieters (myself included) can recite the calorie, carbohydrate, and fat content of foods in great depth and detail, but we are missing a reward to replace the punishment of deprivation and cottage cheese.

Similar situations exist in the world of work. Managers often forget that many jobs involve tasks that are very uncomfortable to perform. In the case of Pro-Products, the plant was hot, dirty, noisy, and often filled with paint fumes. The impact of bells and buzzers would quickly diminish unless additional reinforcement was provided. Since it was physically and economically unfeasible to improve working conditions significantly, economic rewards were suggested through a bonus-incentive plan. Unfortunately, management was unwilling to support such an approach. The result was a return to the previous levels of performance, abandonment of the PA announcements, and the eventual sale of the plant.

To fully understand the process of reinforcement one must also understand its opposite, *extinction*—the disappearance of a learned response. The critical variable is called the reward pattern—that is, how often a reward is attained when performance meets a goal. If rewards are perceived as automatic, they quickly lose their value and thus their power to reinforce behavior. If, on the other hand, rewards are infrequent or random, behavior is much less vulnerable to extinction. This is the power of slot machines; if they paid off every time, players would quickly become bored and stop playing. The challenge, then, is to provide regular, meaningful feedback so that skills will stay sharp while varying rewards enough to keep the game interesting and, more important, the player interested.

Why Training Doesn't Work

The failure of training to produce results is a function of neither technology nor teaching skills, both of which exist in quantity and with quality. The real dilemma is that this failure is only the tip of the learning iceberg; the four issues below the water line (need, practice, feedback, and reinforcement) are much more likely to sink the ship of learning. Their opposites represent the most frequent barriers to skill acquisition. They are:

1. lack of motivation
2. task interference
3. lack of feedback
4. punishment

Most people really do care whether they do a good job. More often than not, people who do not seem to want to learn have been punished for trying. Psychologically people will try harder as they come closer to meeting their needs. If, however, they see little chance of success, they may judge that the effort (cost) isn't worth the trip (value). Practice, feedback, and reinforcement won't work unless the learner can taste success along the way. Good managers of athletes know this and they "bring along" their charges by carefully increasing the level of competition to allow for winning opportunities along the way. Too often, however, business and industry drop their best prospects into the toughest situations with the result that many burn out before they reach their full potential. These incidents, more than anything else, cause learning curves to go flat early.

A second barrier to learning is called task interference. Because learning does not take place in a vacuum, one task may get in the way of learning another. Wimbledon is no place to perfect a backhand; machine operators cannot hone their skills when a customer is screaming for an order; and new managers will not develop leadership skills in the middle of a crisis. That is what practice is for.

The most frequent learning barrier is simply lack of feedback. Indeed, the most common complaint of people at work is that they don't know where they stand. If people can't see the impact of their behavior, the prospect for change is nil. Most human beings are a curious lot and, left to their own devices, will fiddle with a task to see if they can do it better, faster, or more comfortably. This need, when nurtured by providing scorepads, can form the basis for powerful learning experiences.

Finally, there is the case where performing a task is just plain punishing, a situation in which no amount of training will prevent its negative impact. One manager recently expressed shock and dismay upon learning that her customer-service representatives often failed to return calls. "Don't they know that those people [the customers] are our life blood?" she exclaimed. She then proceeded to tick off the possible causes for this inaction: they don't care (lack of motivation), they are too busy (task interference), or they don't realize how important those customers are (lack of feedback).

Because I had been working with the organization for a short time, I already knew that the answer was none of the above. Production had fallen seriously behind schedule, and shipments were running very late. Calls from customers were increasingly irate, and some were becoming downright nasty. Applying Rule 1 (people always act in their own best interest . . .), it was easy to see that returning such calls was a punishing piece of business that quite naturally resulted in avoidance. Once the manager recognized the real problem (Rule 18), she was able to consider two reasonable alternatives: (1) she could get shipments back on schedule; or (2) she could increase the value (rewards) for handling nasty calls, thus reducing the punishment. It is important to note that the customer-service people were quite competent and highly motivated. Quite wisely, they avoided situations that offered no chance for success. Indeed, once the shipment problem was solved, the symptom of slow callbacks disappeared. In contrast, picture how a training program or a series of pep talks would have affected the group (like a lead balloon).

Management Development

A wise old manager once remarked that he could always tell when someone had just returned from a course in human relations because he or she smiled a lot. If the learning of task-related skills is often inadequate, management-skills education is worse. It is either not done or done poorly. Most often the learning of management skills is based on pure trial and error. People are thrown into the water, and those who swim or at least float are the ones who survive. The waste includes both the number that sink to the bottom and those who barely keep their heads above water.

The problems of management development are the flip side of those for management selection. Indeed, training is often an attempt to compensate for poor selection. This is why it is important to distinguish between ability and skill—that is, what can and can't be taught. The most critical ability is insight into one's own and others' behavior. There is no evidence that such a skill can be taught—sharpened, yes, but built from scratch, no. Training a manager who can't "read" people, like teaching algebra to a person who can't add, is an exercise in futility. Consider the following:

> *Rule 28:* An ounce of screening is worth a ton of training.

The problem for trainers is that they have little or no control over who gets tapped for their courses. Such courses are often reserved for those employees who are seen to need them most—in other words, those who can least benefit from the experience because they lack the basic ability. A personal experience with this dynamic may serve to illustrate.

The Zeta Corporation had a problem. The average age of its general managers was 55 and there did not appear to be a clear supply of internal replacements. It was decided to conduct a middle-manager assessment center to identify those who had the potential for such positions (see Chapter 14 for a discussion of the process).

One hundred managers were so identified by the various divisions. After many days of intensive exercises that simulated all aspects of general management, only six were selected by the staff as having the necessary ability. The staff, by the way, was composed solely of the current general managers who had been trained for the task.

In debriefing the staff after the experience, the general managers reached three very significant conclusions. First, many of the 100 middle managers were selected on the basis of availability rather than talent. As the incumbents in the jobs, the general managers were in the best position to know this. They had also gotten a heavy message in terms of the perceived need for such a program. Second, the staff felt they got more out of the experience than did the participants (although many participants did benefit). They felt they had significantly sharpened their skills in identifying talent, which they saw as an important skill in their job. Finally, they noted a huge surge in requests for specific skills training by middle managers who had participated in the program. Thus, as is often true, the process of feedback can lead to the creation of a need. It is particularly noteworthy that requests for training were not the typical "I want to be a better manager" platitudes; rather these requests focused on improving specific skills, such as basic financial planning, marketing, speed-reading, and so on.

The bottom line is that the key to effective management development is to deal with all five steps in the learning process—that is, to (1) ensure that the need for such a process is genuinely felt to be of significant value; (2) train skills that are relevant and teachable to those who have the ability to master them; (3) provide opportunities to practice skills on the job; (4) provide accurate, timely feedback; and (5) create opportunities for success as new skills are acquired.

Conclusions

Right up there with the chicken and the egg is the debate about whether managers are born or made. Central to one's argument is whether the function is seen as an art or a science. Forced to choose, I would have to opt for art. Like painting or sculpting, one must have *both* ability and skill to achieve results. The power of education is to endow those who have the ability with the skills to get the job done. Few people outside of the art world know that for all of Picasso's free-flowing innovation he was first an excellent technician; he could sketch pictures with such realism that it was difficult to distinguish them from photographs.

The most provocative question in management development is why more isn't done. The answer may well be Rule 1. Consider the reality of a manager who is told that he should "develop his people." If he believes this and puts energy into sharpening the skills of those with the most ability, he may well lose them to other organizations. His "reward" for that effort becomes the "opportunity" to recruit and select replacements at his own department's expense.

Two solutions seem apparent. One is to create a reward system for those who develop managers; a way to do this is to hold managers accountable for the competence of their replacements. The other is to identify those with potential early in their careers and nurture them with the same care given to dollars and dump trucks.

PART VI

STRATEGY

They are playing a game. They are playing at not playing a game. If I show them I see they are, I shall break the rules and they will punish me. I must play the game, of not seeing that I play the game.

R. D. Laing

17

People

*People in glass houses shouldn't
throw stones.* Famous architect

The game of management does not require an understanding of human behavior and performance to play. First and foremost, managers must know their business. Indeed, without a reasonable level of technical competence, a manager is most likely doomed to failure or at least mediocrity. But insight into people does provide an edge—one that can spell the difference between winning and losing. The problem is that organizations tend to exaggerate the level of technical expertise required and to underestimate the people-oriented skills needed. The net result is a clear fix on content but a blind eye to process. This is how organizations lose sight of what business they are in; they see the trees but miss the forest.

Again, then, here are the five rules that relate to why people do what they do:

Rule 1: People always act in their own best interest, given the facts as they know them.

Rule 2: People act to meet perceived needs.

Rule 3: People meet needs by getting rewards and avoiding punishment.

Rule 11: People do not behave logically; they behave psychologically.

Rule 17: People rarely fail for technical reasons.

Managers commonly complain that employees do not act the way they are *supposed* to act, and this "bad acting" is often labeled with terms like poor attitude, laziness, or negative thinking. Such labeling or libeling is a trap. Since it rests on the assumption that something is wrong with the people, the solution tends to focus on changing them. The trap is that it can't be done, not their genes, nor their chromosomes, nor their personality. This is the bad news.

The good news is that such change is not really necessary. Since a manager's true aim is to achieve results, all that is required is performance change. Such change may require a modification of people's behavior, but *they* will do that if they perceive it to be in their best interests. Thus, a manager's job is to create situations that will guide people to such perceptions.

The above is so easily provable that one must wonder why so few managers accept it. The answer lies in assumption of fault. If an employee's poor performance is a result of some character flaw, then the manager is relatively blameless. If, on the other hand, the cause of such performance is situational, then the manager must be accountable. To set the record straight, consider Rule 29.

> *Rule 29:* Bad performance is caused by bad manage-
> ment, not by bad people.

Even in those rare cases where an employee is truly incorrigible, management must take responsibility for hiring such people, placing them, and keeping them on the payroll.

Managers Are People

So many books on management seem to draw such a sharp distinction between boss and subordinate that one might wonder if they are different species. But managers are people, too, and their behavior follows the same patterns as those they supervise. The difference is that managers who are truly effective must come out from behind their defenses and see themselves as others do. This does not mean they must change, only that they must know the impact they have on others. Without interpersonal feedback, one can never distinguish between what works and what doesn't work. Take this case as an example.

Rod was a bright, aggressive manager who had moved up the corporate ladder quickly but seemed to have reached a plateau. When he participated in a company assessment center designed to identify future top managers, he had the opportunity to get a great deal of feedback from his fellow participants as well as from the staff of general managers. To a person, they told him he was an arrogant SOB who acted with little or no sensitivity to other people's feelings.

At the end of the week-long program, Rod met with me and argued that the group was absolutely wrong about their assessment of him. He insisted that they were weak and probably jealous of his success. Since it was pointless to argue with him, I suggested he mull over what had taken place and call me in a few weeks to discuss it further.

It was nearly a month later when Rod called. He told me that he had further proof that the assessment of him had been incorrect. Soon after he returned home, he had called his staff together and put it to them point-blank. "Am I an arrogant SOB?" he demanded. "No, sir!" they chimed in unison. "So you see," Rod continued, "you people were all wrong about me."

If Rod had not sounded so serious, I would not have been able to suppress a massive giggling fit. Instead, I decided to try to get through to him one more time. After acknowledging that he might very well be right, I suggested that he give the matter one more test. "Tonight when you go home, Rod, share the feedback you got here with your wife and ask her if it fits," I instructed. He agreed.

The next morning a message was waiting for me. It simply read: "How did you know?—Rod." As I told him in later conversations, feedback is a gift, not a weapon. Only a person who loves you or at least cares about you will risk telling you what you don't want to hear.

Defense Mechanisms

Human beings are born into this world helpless and dependent. In order to survive, they need to lean on others. Children learn to depend on their parents not only for physical comforts but also for the comfort of approval. The search for approval continues into adulthood. In the approval of others, people are reassured of their own worth. So great is the need for approval, in fact, that people will deceive themselves rather than face reality; they are protecting the image they have of themselves. Such protection usually takes shape in one of four forms:

1. rationalization
2. projection
3. displacement
4. compensation

The most common form of defense is *rationalization*. Starting with the image we need for ourselves, we build a case through a series of "rational" explanations. This is why it was hopeless to argue with Rod. Indeed, it is to his credit that he was willing to accept his wife's feedback. He could just as easily have argued that his behavior at home was different than it was at work. Never try to win an argument with rationalizers. Their "false perceptions" are their protection against losing. Instead, if you want to help them to see themselves more clearly, find our first if *they* truly want to. Then help them set up a plan to do so.

Projection is a more difficult defense mechanism to deal with. People who use it disown the problem and place it on the other guy. To break through, one must clarify ownership—that is, identify who has the problem. A manager who goes to a subordinate and says, "You have a problem," is sure to face a stone wall. In the subordinate's mind the natural reaction is, "I didn't have a problem until you walked in, so *you* are the problem." An alternate approach is to begin the dialogue with, "I have a problem and I need your help." The "problem" may be the subordinate's performance, but it will never be resolved while the two parties stand on opposite sides of a wall.

Displacement is the process of accepting one's faults but blaming others for their existence. Such behavior most often takes the form, "I would be more successful if only they would. . . ." Such a defense is easier to deal with, since the people do recognize they are at fault. The key is to get them to assume full reponsibility for their own circumstances. Such is the nature of people giving up their power (see Rule 9).

A fourth defense is *compensation,* or emphasizing an area of strength to make up for an area of weakness. On the surface, compensation seems to make logical sense. But often it just doesn't work out that way. For example, a strong emphasis on technical expertise will not compensate for a lack of people-oriented skills if the problem is people. Likewise, superb people-oriented skills will not counterbalance a lack of technical skill if the problem is technical.

Managing Defensive Behavior

Psychological defense mechanisms are sets of automatic responses that people develop to protect themselves. They are just as natural as the release of adrenaline or clenching of muscles when faced with a physical threat. Managers who cannot deal with such behavior will be doomed to a lifetime of unresolved conflict in their organization.

Perhaps the most important key is to focus on performance, not on behavior. If you must criticize, criticize the act rather than the person. Further, never confront a person's defenses unless you want a fight. All people make excuses for themselves at times; such behavior is normal and healthy. If you can see behind people's masks and understand why they behave the way they do, use that insight to help them meet their needs in more productive ways. If you have the skill to do this, you will have a small edge in the game of management.

Self-Awareness

If you have ever seen yourself on videotape, you know what a shock it can be. If we can be so unaware of our physical appearance, is it any wonder that we are so blind to our feelings, emotions, beliefs, values, and goals? People fail in life for the same reason organizations fail. They don't know what business they are in! To find out, one must go through a diagnostic process similar to the one described for organizations in Chapter 9. The major elements are:

1. History: where have you been?
2. Analysis: what did you learn?
3. Goals: where are you going?
4. Needs: why do you want to be there?
5. Barriers: what stands in your way?

What a person remembers about his or her childhood and youth is significant precisely because it is remembered. A person's memory can provide great insight into what he or she continues to consider important or trivial. Childhood memories are a window to an adult's values. In the classic film *Citizen Kane*, the central character is a powerful billionaire who seems to have achieved everything yet remains unhappy. On his deathbed, his last word is "Rosebud," the name of his beloved childhood sled.

History is significant because we learn what is of value. But for most people, this learning is not at a conscious level. The Depression children who placed great importance on frugality and avoiding risk have been replaced by inflation-era children who see wisdom in buying now and borrowing to the hilt. Either extreme will greatly influence how a person behaves as a manager or a subordinate. Also, early relationships with parents, siblings, and friends will greatly affect how a person will deal with others during his or her adult-hood.

To enhance self-awareness, a useful technique is to write an autobiographical sketch. Then ask someone you know and trust to read it and comment on what appears to be significant. The two keys to this diagnosis are *focus* (writing it down) and *feedback* (how others see you). You may be surprised to learn that the most significant data are those small details that stay with you and recur ✓ whenever you think about the past.

The hardest part of increasing self-awareness is in articulating goals. Most people just don't plan their lives or their careers; fully 90 percent of the people I have met are in careers that developed through fate and circumstance! Also, just as the profit motive is often a myth for organizations, so is the money motive for individuals. It's what they *do* with the money that has importance.

To gain greater insight, people should explore not only where they are going but why they want to be there. If a person really *needs* to make a lot of money, he or she would do well to explore what jobs offer the best chance for doing so. As a test, try this exercise:

> *You have just learned that you have six months to live. You will suffer no pain, and all of your financial obligations have been taken care of. In addition, you have $50,000 to spend as you please. How will you use the time? Write out your answer.*

This brief exercise can yield profound insights into your goals and values. If your answer reveals that you would make significant changes in how you spend your time, several important questions are raised. For example, why aren't you occupying yourself in that way now? Or why aren't you working toward goals that would enable you to do so? This exercise can also sharpen your understanding of the barriers that exist between where you are and where you are going. It is surprising to many people that money is rarely the barrier. For instance, I learned that an entrepreneur I was working with felt very guilty about the small amount of time he spent with his family. Using the exercise, he was able to conclude, "In the future I doubt if I will spend more time with my family, *but* I will feel less guilty." Thus, the barrier was not time but guilt. His original rationalization was that he was making pots of money for his family. What changed was his acceptance that it was *he*, not his family, who needed greater wealth.

Locus of Control

One aspect of people's values—their locus of control—requires special attention. The term *locus of control* refers to whether a person sets internal or external standards. People who have an outer locus of control are those who continue to need affirmation of their self-worth. They are the ones who *need* big desks, deep pile carpets, and corner offices. In contrast is the rare individual who possesses an inner locus of control. Marching to a different drummer, such a person *knows* inside what is right and what is wrong. Such folks make great entrepreneurs, good sales reps, and awful bureaucrats.

Most people fall somewhere in between these extremes. It is vital for managers to know where they stand with respect to control. An inner locus of control will not guarantee the success of a new venture, but an outer locus of control will almost certainly lead to failure. Consider this organizational example.

The Snappy Snack Food Company is headquartered in Sarasota, Florida. A new general manager was needed for the potato-chip plant in Blue Buns, North Dakota. Three hot-shot assistant plant managers were offered the job, and each one turned it down. The vice-president was furious at their lack of ambition, not to mention their "disloyalty." Since I knew the situation, I suggested he look at the opportunity from the candidates' point of view. The Blue Buns facility was filled with antiquated equipment, and it was poorly positioned in the marketplace. The board of directors had recently voted not to put any more money into it. On top of all of that, the three candidates lived in the Sunbelt; they didn't have a pair of snow tires among them. They knew the risks involved in turning down the opportunity, but they also saw the probability for payoff too slim to take the chance.

Once the vice-president was able to see the general manager's job from the candidate's perspective, he was quickly able to identify the problem as a high-risk, turnaround situation that was going to reward success with the opportunity to stay in the freezer section of the U.S. His solution was to offer the job to a top-performing plant manager who was two years from retirement. The deal included free living expenses in Blue Buns, relocation back home in two years, and a modest salary increase that would affect his final retirement pay. Not only did the man accept the deal, but the three assistant managers fought for the opportunity to take his old job.

The vice-president learned that opportunity and risk, like beauty, are in the eye of the beholder. It is the essence of Rule 11 (people do not behave logically . . .). Perceived risk depends on a person's values and locus of control (. . . they behave psychologically).

A Small Edge

What a good game player looks for is an edge, no matter how small, that will tip the balance away from pure chance. Every professional athlete knows that the difference between winning and losing is often a fraction of an inch or a tenth of a second. The same is true of the management game. If you compare an effective manager with one who is not, you will see few major differences in their behavior. It's the small things, the critical incidents, that separate the winners from the losers. Here are ten tips that can give a manager that vital edge:

1. listen
2. know the job
3. know the people

4. know the game
5. critical incidents
6. acceptance
7. change
8. time
9. limits
10. help

A manager's greatest enemy is surprise. Although few crises develop overnight, many seem to do so because few of us hear or want to hear the early warning signals. As a consultant who often walks into such crises, I am continually amazed by how deaf people can be when they don't want to hear bad news. This reveals how strong defense mechanisms can be. If a manager is concerned about "communications problems," he or she would do well to rephrase this: "How do I stop myself from hearing and seeing what is going on?" Listening skill is the radar that provides the basis of management control. It's a small edge that can mean a big difference in terms of results.

A second edge can be gained by knowing the jobs that need to be done—not the puffery of position descriptions, but the results that are expected. There is a top-seeded tennis player who holds her racket "wrong," but no one complains because she wins. There are sales reps who do not fit their company's executive image but are tolerated because they exceed their quotas. A manager who looks at function first and form second is one who has a distinct game advantage.

The related issue of knowing the people in the organization is also important to a manager. Management skill is the "shock absorber" between the inflexibility of an organization's structure and the widely divergent needs of the people it employs. A wise manager is one who has clear insight into the strengths and weaknesses of subordinates. He or she needs to know what turns them on and off. Many a manager remains ignorant of subordinates' outside activities because he or she is afraid of becoming personally involved in their lives. The fact of the matter is, though, that there is no way a boss can avoid being a significant influence in these people's lives. The payoff for aloofness is a greater level of comfort in maintaining discipline. But the risks of dealing blindly with people are just not worth it. A top salesperson wouldn't dream of making a presentation to a prospective customer without first finding out as much as he or she could about the people who make the buying decisions. Yet that same person will manage a sales territory without the foggiest notion of what makes the reps tick. Management is the orchestration of talent on board. Anybody can win with superstars three deep in every position. But the true test of a manager's skill is to make the best of what he or she has got.

The secret to knowing the game you are playing translates into pace and purpose. No human being will give 100 percent all the time. A good hitter in baseball knows when to swing for the fences and when to just meet the ball. Tennis players who go for an ace every time had better have a great second serve. A good manager will have a firm grasp on Pareto's Law, knowing which few actions will have the greatest impact on results. A manager who demands excellence in everything will not get people's best effort. To get an edge, one must teach people when to drop the hammer and when to coast. If not, people will develop their own pace and may well put their best efforts into trivia.

To do the above, a manager must have insight into those critical incidents that result in a big payoff. It is not enough to know the game; a manager must also be able to distinguish between the big plays and the milk runs. I recall the manager of a company cafeteria who brought order out of chaos through much planning and considerable structure. One change was to close the facility promptly at 1:30, rather than letting people linger at their tables until midafternoon. When an employee barred the president from entering at 1:35, the manager almost lost his job.

With the possible exception of brain surgeons and airline

pilots, an employee's mistake is rarely fatal. It is vital that subordinates feel a sense of acceptance and approval. A manager who condemns errors indiscriminately is destined to live with mediocrity. If employees can change and it's important, help them. If they must change but can't, hollering won't help; they must go.

The most significant question a manager can ask is *when*. By definition a manager must delegate responsibility downward in the organization. Without a timetable, he or she has no control and is asking for trouble. A timetable provides key bench marks that enable positive action to be taken when problems begin to crop up. It's another way to avoid surprise. Also, it allows people to work at their own pace. Some will get the job done right away, others will "cram" at the last minute. Either way, people perform better when given a deadline. They work best when they participate in setting it.

As was pointed out in Chapter 16, training is often expected to produce miracles; it is but one case of impossible expectations that ignore people's capabilities. Managers must know the limits to their own as well as to their subordinates' talents. A person can stretch just so far, and potential is no guarantee that people will live up to it. One part of accepting individuals and their uniqueness is to be aware of their limitations as well as their strengths. If people haven't performed at a particular level in the past, they aren't likely to in the future. This may be a hard reality to accept, but to ignore it is to lose that small edge.

Last but not least, a manager must know when to ask for help. Perhaps it's all that military jargon, but many organizations continue to promote a macho image in which asking for help is a sign of weakness. Professional athletes are surrounded by experts ranging from coaches and trainers to hypnotists. A professional manager should be equally open to the use of such experts. Edges are hard enough to come by without worrying about one's image. Let your results speak for themselves. If they aren't heard, then the game is crooked. If the name of the game is really *image*, then learn to project a winning one. Get an image expert.

Conclusions

A manager is not expected to be a magician or a mind reader. He or she is an orchestrator who must achieve results through the efforts of a group of imperfect human beings. The opportunity is there for those who choose to listen and act. The challenge is to keep honing skills by seeking and finding a small edge.

18

Process

If you can't stand the heat, stay out of the kitchen. Famous chef

A manager's role is to achieve desired results (Rule 7). To do this he or she is expected to plan, organize, direct, and control an organization with some degree of effectiveness. And to do this, in turn, one must understand how individuals, groups, and organizations function. The complexity of such functioning is further compounded and confounded by the nearly infinite array of interrelationships between the three.

Management is a game because the players are trying to predict outcomes in an environment of uncertainty. If such outcomes were purely random, then management skill would be a myth and there would be no need for this book. On the other hand, if events could be precisely predicted, there would be no need for managers; they could and should be replaced with robots. Fortunately, neither is the case. The game of management involves a constant battle with uncertainty. Effective control is knowing what to do before an event occurs, *regardless* of the outcome. The process is called planning.

A good poker player does not expect to win every hand any more than a good salesperson expects to close every prospect. But both do know how to take maximum advantage of any situation, which is the essence of control and the validation of the planning process. The focus of this chapter will be on how a manager can achieve control through planning.

Planning

The trouble with most organizational plans is that they are too content-oriented, all words and no music. They are created in a vacuum that assumes a whole host of ideal conditions. Anyone holding a royal flush can win a hand of poker; the real challenge is to take a pot with a pair of deuces. Effectiveness is measured by how well you do with what you've got. One must read people as well as cards, assessing human resources as well as technical ones. Planning is the process by which the target is defined. Without a plan there is no control, and the player is at the mercy of fate and circumstance. His or her only hope for winning is dumb blind luck. In contrast, a skilled player is one who is in control even when the cards are bad. To be in control is to see and understand what is going on.

The power to see things the way they really are rests with one's point of view. A machinist would never try to make a part without at least three drawings (top, front, and side). A manager, too, must be able to see his or her organization from different perspectives. Unlike a blueprint, however, the congruence between views is less than perfect. Such is the measure of uncertainty that makes management a game, its targets glass, and the process critical.

Planning must take into account uncertainty. An organizational plan is not a blueprint but rather a road map that tries to present all alternatives and a "best" course of action. When a dead end is reached, one is able to make a U-turn and try again. If a manager or a driver has only a set of instructions, then one wrong turn will result in becoming lost. The essence of control, then, is having a map. Previous chapters have tried to pick out points of interest. Now we will try to put together the entire layout.

An Organizational Map

Organizations are systems that involve three components: input, output, and process. They take resources, transform them, and yield results. (See Figure 17.) Because managers live within their

Figure 17. **An organizational map.**

Resources (Input) →	Strategy (Process) →	Results (Output)
People	Tasks	Performance
Places	Talent	Growth
Things	Structure	Charge

own process, they tend to take a myopic view and look inward. This is a trap because process is *defined* by resources and results. There is no strategy that is inherently good or bad in and of itself. A good plan is one that puts you in the right place at the right time. A good manager is one who knows what to do when he or she gets there.

Organizations are complex systems by definition. It is tempting, therefore, to design complex maps to describe them. The problem is that as complexity increases, understanding decreases, so that one quickly reaches a point of diminishing returns. One need not memorize a table of probabilities to play poker well, but it is essential to know a good hand from a bad one. An awful player always draws to an inside straight, a fair player never does, and a good player will do so only when the situation is right (if the pot is big enough to warrant such a long shot). But a great player knows when to stand pat on such a hand and bluff. This goes beyond playing cards; it is playing the other people at the table.

An organizational map can make a good manager great, and it can even make a fair manager good. It will not, however, help a poor manager because he or she will not know what to do on arrival. A map is of no use to a person who is still trying to figure out how to work the gear shift. Here, then, is a simplistic but hopefully understandable guide to achieving results.

Resources

Organizations fail when they don't know what business they are in (Rule 10). Such failure is most often due to mistaken assumptions about the nature of available resources. Organizations exist to survive (Rule 6). How they survive becomes part of their past history and thus their present culture. It is said that those who do not learn from the past are destined to repeat it. Too often, however, history is seen as a mere chronicle of events. In fact, the learning is not in the events (content) but in the strategy (process) of a group's past interactions with the environment. The norms and values that emerge are of the greatest importance.

To understand an organization's resources is to be a bit of an anthropologist. The culture of an organization is determined by people, places, and things. The type of person who is attracted to a particular organization says much about its perceived environment. Much has been written about paternalism in organizations, for example, but little is said about the needs of people who are attracted to such a culture. Fatherly managers cannot exist without childlike subordinates.

Buildings, too, reflect the nature of organizations. Offices and factories range from the sumptuous to the squalid. The key is not the level of elegance of such places but how the décor "fits" with the culture. Of particular note should be any evidence of groups split into the "haves" and the "have-nots," as is often the case when a manufacturing facility is physically connected to an office complex.

A third set of resources is the tools organizations employ to accomplish tasks. These may range from managerial toys to state-of-the-art technology. Here, too, fit is of the utmost significance. Some organizations try to shovel fertilizer with a teaspoon, while others dig in sandboxes with bulldozers. The incongruence says much about the values and norms of the organization.

People

Managers freely admit that the level of talent in an organization is its most significant resource—one that will more often spell the difference between success and failure than will places or things. Yet their actions in plant start-ups, mergers, and takeovers show that organizations give most attention to buildings and equipment. Consider the following typical and often-repeated scenario.

The Slam-Bang Swinging Door Company was started by Sam and Sarah Slam in their basement. Through hard work and Sam's genius for designing special-purpose portals, the company grew and prospered. After more than a quarter of a century, the Slams sold out to the Consolidated Construction Corporation. It was a sweet deal for Sam and Sarah, who got cash and stock and leased back the building, which they owned. For Consolidated the deal appeared equally tasty, as the products and customers fit nicely with their overall marketing strategy. Forthwith they deployed their boy-wonder staff expert to run the place.

It took less than eight months for the wheels to fall off. In the first quarter it was "discovered" that the business did not really make much of a profit; the Slams had used the business to shelter income and had carried cars, homes, and kids on the books. They drew a modest salary but paid themselves a handsome rental on the property. Consolidated had to pay substantially bigger salaries for the new managers as well as the same building rent. In addition, the plant was saddled with a corporate assessment that threatened to turn the bottom line red.

These data could and should have been uncovered by the Consolidated auditors. What did not appear on any financial statements, however, was the quality of management in the organization. Sam was a genius but also a benevolent autocrat; he made all the decisions. The young president of Consolidated inherited a cadre of people who were long on technical experience but very short on accepting responsibility. In essence, he had to rebuild the organizational structure from the ground up, and in the process he replaced almost every manager. The cost was staggering, wiping out the assumed benefit of buying an already existing business.

An organization is like a tapestry woven from the unique resources available to it; pluck out the wrong thread and the whole business can unravel. On the other hand, a good fit can provide strength far greater than the sum of individual talent. The ability to survive the loss of any one member is intrinsic to organizations (Rule 5) and distinguishes them from one-man bands.

If a manager is to have an edge in achieving results, he or she must learn to assess talent and understand how such resources are combined in work groups. It is not enough to know that the structure works; one must understand why. A good test is to take the organization chart and erase the names. If it makes functional sense, there is some likelihood that resources are being efficiently managed. On the other hand, if it appears cumbersome and confusing, there may well be a fundamental defect in the fabric.

Places and Things

House hunting is a fascinating experience because one has an opportunity to examine the physical shell of a family without the distraction of personalities, puppy dogs, and paraphernalia. One quickly gets a feel for what is valued and what is not.

The same is true for the physical structure within which organizations operate. People cannot help but leave their imprint on the places they live and work. When the environment is sterile, so will be the human interaction. If it is in great disrepair, attempts to produce quality work will be severely handicapped. There is a texture to the psychological environment of workplaces, and it is easy to see if one is not distracted.

Not much of significance has been written about the physical surroundings of work. Yet for people whose locus of control is external, the impact of the work environment can be substantial. Studies of light, color, and sound miss the forest for the trees. Proponents of office landscaping and offices without walls rarely take into consideration the norms and values an organization places on such structures before they begin distributing dividers and potted palms. Still, such planning is light-years ahead of the typical approach to factory layouts, where people are often accommodated as a reluctant afterthought.

Having conducted dozens of organizational-climate surveys, I continue to be struck by the significance put on places and things. Seen through the eyes of top management they are trivial. But for those who sweat for a living, little things mean a lot. The single most frequent request of assembly-line workers is permission to bring a radio, and more productivity has been lost due to a broken soda machine than will ever be imagined.

Top management is not immune from such issues either. The griping over office décor, parking places, and company cars can get downright nasty. To deal with such behavior on a logical basis is to miss the point. This is psychological stuff that has the issues of power and stress at its core. The powerless worker wants a measure of comfort to compensate for the dull routine and constant pressure to perform; the powerful boss wants to maintain the perception of power through the possession of the appropriate places and things.

Effectiveness is often an outcome of the integration of individual needs and organizational goals. All organizations achieve some balance between the two that is less than perfect. The degree of good fit tends to be a major determinant of how much stress is created. Discrepancies between people and their environment will often focus on places and things rather than people. Think about it: are people "squeezed" into an organization, or has it been designed to fit them? Since managers cannot change people's personalities, they would be well advised to consider the dynamics of congruence. Slam-Bang fit Sam like a glove, but it did not fit Consolidated at all. Such is the message of Rule 20 (when in doubt, leave it alone). Before you tinker with an organization, know *why* it works. The bright young man from Consolidated who once flew with eagles now finds himself amid a gaggle of geese.

Strategy

Strategy is the organizational "black box" that converts resources into results. It is axiomatic that organizations can tolerate considerable error in detail if their overall strategy is correct. Such process involves consideration of tasks, talent, and structure.

In the broad sense, all organizations have a strategy or basic transformation process. Although some strategies are planned, many are the result of history and growth. Over time, the essence of an organization can be lost or forgotten. Change is inevitable yet few plan for it, which is why organizations that do not grow often die.

The difference between winning and losing in the long run rests on management's *awareness* of strategy and process. The time to consider consolidation of gains and conservative approaches is the early years of organizational adolescence, when the trap lies in over-extending. On the other hand, the time to take risks and innovate is when the business has matured or is entering old age. Too often organizations behave quite the opposite, risking all in the early years and tightening up at twilight.

As organizations grow, there is a natural tendency for systems to face inward, which results in management's losing sight of the original purpose of the organization. This internal focus causes overly tight control and prohibits creativity. In contrast is the rare organization that develops an external focus, which more often than not results in successful adaptation to changes in markets and technologies.

On the surface these results would seem to contradict Rule 15 (when you are winning, don't change the game), but the key is to differentiate between the total game and a single hand. In Chapter 6, we described an organizational life cycle that runs from birth to death. On closer examination, though, organizations can survive indefinitely *if* they keep growing and changing. That is, while a single product or service has a finite life span, new products and services can keep the organization young and vibrant.

To survive indefinitely requires an external focus, which does not occur naturally. The inherent tendency of groups is to maintain order (Rule 4), leading to systems that encourage a preoccupation with internal functioning. When this disposition is taken to its extreme, a bureaucracy results.

It is possible to create an external focus, but such an undertaking requires system change. Such change must be introduced from the outside (Rule 21) and will be reflected in how tasks, talent, and structure are dealt with.

Tasks

The tasks of management that most closely relate to helping an organization grow are reflected in three areas: *risk taking, reality testing,* and *number punching.* The natural overcontrol of systems and the eventual obsession with detail can so punish risk taking as to make it extinct. To flourish over the long haul, an organization must *manage risk* by supporting experimentation. It is simply outrageous how little comfort is given to those who wish to try something new and different.

An even more devastating example of overcontrol is lack of realistic goals and objectives. One game that corporations play is establishing targets and making forecasts that the field finds impossible to achieve. Such activities fly in the face of everything we know about goal setting and human performance; the essence of effective goal setting is based on achievable targets and participation by those who must achieve them. A goal that requires "stretch" does indeed result in increased performance, much like the "kick" at the end of a distance race. As people near their objective, their level of motivation increases as they push to break the tape at the finish line. However, when the target is too far away or impossible to attain, frustration sets in to the point that performance suffers greatly.

It is *short-term* not long-term planning that is the key to attaining goals. A five-year plan is a nice idea, but if an organization can't predict monthly performance such a plan will be an exercise in futility. The lesson for management is that if you can't hit the broadside of a barn, leave your telescopic sight at home.

The relationship between risk taking and reality testing is a close one. Realistic organizations foster and support managed risk because there is a sense of predictability. That is, the numbers are good and thus short-term forecasts tend to be fairly accurate. But when systems do not fit reality there is an atmosphere of mistrust and suspicion that precludes risk taking. The result is a culture that plays it safe and stunts organizational growth.

A third management task area is that of number punching. Here, too, overcontrol can stifle growth by suffocating risk-taking behavior. Organizations that track dozens of different variables end up in "paralysis by analysis." Line organizations become bewildered as to which targets are important—a prime example of system overload in which many data are transmitted but little real information is communicated. The answer is to establish a few sharply focused numbers that can provide the framework for active risk taking and solid reality testing.

Structure

In Chapter 2, structure was shown to be a function of goals, values, and norms. In that context, the difference between formal and informal structure takes on a whole new meaning. Traditional definitions tend to equate "informal" with "unpredictable." In actual fact, though, the issue at hand is whether the organization is focusing on values and norms (knowing what business you are in) or on policies and procedures (form replacing function). The key element in both outlooks is the quality and texture of goals. A target of a 20-percent sales increase looks inward and can easily lead to negotiation of quotas by sales managers that are as low as possible; this system *encourages* risk reduction. On the other hand, a goal of increasing market share by 2 percent encourages an external focus, and managers will be more likely—though not certain—to focus on values and norms. In other words, not only will they establish where they are going but how they will get there. Such a process supports risk taking more because it is more realistic and thus more predictable.

Talent

It has already been pointed out that the ability to identify and develop talent provides a manager with an edge in the game of management. To *keep* that edge, a manager must put equal effort into maintaining that talent. It is not enough to put the right people in the right spots. Such talent must be nurtured, or it will go to seed like an untended garden.

Nowhere is this point more important than in the care and feeding of top-performing, key managers. Their talent is rare and forms the very foundation of organizational strategy. Yet too often they are either taken for granted or ignored. The most significant strategic norm an organization can develop is the value placed on management talent. Tasks and structure can be quickly changed, but not talent.

Lest one get the impression that maintaining management talent is synonymous with compensation, it should be added that such is not the case. Rather, the issue is one of timing. If a key manager is performing well, give that person more and do it now. If she is doing poorly, give her help and do it quickly. If the situation is hopeless, cut her loose. This is the essence of Rule 30.

Rule 30: Never delay decisions about people.

Results

Throughout this book, great emphasis has been placed on process with the intent to counterbalance the traditional overconcern for content. To be effective, a manager must be tuned in to both the words and the music, which is the message of Rule 31.

Rule 31: Never accept a result that is all numbers.

Every level of an organization between a manager and where work actually takes place acts as a filter that distorts information. Thus, numbers alone cannot tell the whole story. Consider this case.

Slicko Sockets sells and services tools and hardware for the auto-repair business. Profits had plummeted in recent years, and a new national sales manager was hired to turn the tide. At the national sales meeting he announced that prices and sales quotas would be increased. He also relieved sales managers of their authority to make pricing decisions. By taking command and centralizing control, he hoped to bring the numbers back to healthy levels. Indeed, for the next 12 months profits did increase.

However, there were also a number of distressing side effects. Turnover tripled, the morale of the sales force reached a low ebb, and a few sales managers left the company to start competing firms. The national sales manager found himself living on the telephone with no time to plan or organize. The numbers were getting better, but the staff's feelings were not. At this point, I was asked to lend a hand.

My diagnosis revealed a number of startling facts. First, less than 10 percent of the sales force was making quota. Second, those that were hitting their targets were in markets where price was not the primary determinant in buying decisions. Third, many of the successful sales reps were violating company policy in order to make sales. For example, one rep "bootlegged" tools to give away to new customers who placed large orders.

Upon my return to corporate headquarters, I asked the national sales manager to summarize his experience with the company. He told me that when he came on board he found an organization that was out of control. "Salesmen were giving away the store," he said. "We were selling a large volume of items at a loss."

His diagnosis was correct, but his problem definition was not. Salespeople were selling at a loss because it was in their best interest to do so (Rule 1); commissions were based on sales dollars not profit. Taking pricing decisions away from the sales managers did stop this practice, but it was also undermining the sales managers' authority. The system was not working because there was no clear-cut strategy. Bandages had stopped the bleeding, but the organization was on the verge of hemorrhaging.

The solutions were threefold. First, targets were reset in terms of profit. Second, quotas were made tough but attainable; they were regionalized to better reflect the significant differences among markets. Third, the problem of pricing authority was redefined as salesmanager effectiveness. A sales manager who could not be trusted with pricing decisions was in the wrong job. In one fell swoop, issues of tasks, talent, and structure were dealt with. The numbers aren't in yet, but the odds of success are significantly better.

Performance, Growth, and Change

Results are a function of performance, growth, and change. The single greatest barrier to good performance is inertia. "We've done it this way for years, why change?" Such is the rationale for poor planning. Planning is important, and it is tedious. As the saying goes, there is never time to do it right but always time to do it over. But first and foremost, a manager must be prepared to step up to the plate and swing. No one can hit the ball from the dugout.

To succeed is to grow, not to grow is to die, and there is nothing in between. The key is change. Results will not change unless the situation is changed. If performance is lousy someone is accepting mediocrity. Go for excellence—not perfection, mind you, but excellence. If excellent performance does not achieve the result you want, you are in the wrong game.

It takes time to turn a situation around; that is the bad news. The good news is that it takes an equal amount of time for things to go sour. Effective organizations can define their strategies on a single sheet of paper; they watch a few numbers closely; they pay similarly close attention to their top managers; they move planning and control functions down, not up. These are the secrets to acting quickly. Overcontrol, in contrast, results in *reacting*—in other words, swinging at the ball after it's in the catcher's glove.

19

Style

When the going gets tough, the tough get going. Famous travel agent

In Chapter 4 the role of manager was described in terms of four functions: planning, organizing, directing, and controlling. Like the movement of chess pieces, these functions describe the game, not how to play. A second dimension that reflects pure process is needed. This is *management style*.

Classical theorists have argued that managers should adopt a style that maximizes the above functions. Like an off-the-rack suit, such approaches assume off-the-rack bodies—a good theory that falls apart in practice. More recently, such scholars have proposed that an effective manager's behavior is appropriate to the circumstances; this implies the use of different styles in different settings—sort of an "alterations included" approach with a nip here and a tuck there to reflect the specific nature of the people, the tasks, and the boss-subordinate relationships. These contingency approaches assume that managers can alter their behavior at will, but most often they can't—a strong argument, by the way, for management selection based on fit.

The dilemma of a conceptualized management style is that the focus is once again on behavior rather than on performance. Even those models that include alterations ultimately seek to classify the manager's behavior into standard shapes and sizes. The contingent manager is expected to quickly assess the situation (locate the target), select the "right" style out of his or her repertoire (choose the weapon), and take action (pull the trigger). Certainly it is good to become more aware of one's behavior, and practicing new variations of style can add to the richness of a manager's skill and increase the depth and breadth of his or her ability. However, on the firing line a manager's primary behavior will be based on intuition. There are just too many hard observable data and too much sound psychological research pointing to the near impossibility of changing major habit patterns. Such changes definitely will not take place as the result of complex conceptualizations. What is needed are a few key bench marks that can help managers quickly sight a target and tell them when to pull the trigger. Functions alone may define the style but what is missing is action—that is, *what* to do and *when* to do it. The following story may serve to illustrate the dilemma of the textbook manager who is long on theory but short on practice.

Harvey B. School was the recipient of a freshly minted M.B.A. He was hired as the general manager of a business that was in serious trouble. He spent his first few days meeting the people and touring the facility. Finally he called his staff into the conference room and said, "O.K., give me the case."

Management's Three Responses

As mentioned previously, the secret to problem solving is in definition (Rule 18). Too often managers have difficulty in even locating the problem; they tend to see only what is put in front of them. Somehow they need to break out of the system flow with its homogenized prepackaged proposals and see the targets more clearly.

When a manager faces a situation that needs managing, he or she will respond in one of three ways: reaction, proaction, or interaction. These are the choices if any action is going to take place. Combined with the four management functions, we can illustrate the broad arena within which results will be achieved by the accompanying table.

The Management Arena

Function	Style		
	React	Proact	Interact
Plan	by habit	by map	by compass
Organize	by task	by situation	by mission
Direct	to opportunity	to goals	to values
Control	through power	through achievement	through affiliation

Complex treatises on management style, like trying to tell a tennis player how to hit the ball, are an exercise in futility. Indeed, such books as *Inner Tennis* point to how improved skills can be achieved much more significantly by focusing on the result rather than on the behavior—that is, visualizing the ball going over the net rather than the complex eye-hand coordination required.

In management, as in tennis, style determines the way in which you will confront the ball (target); there is no time to make such a choice once it's in play. In tennis the choices are to hit the ball flat, with a slice, or with a top spin. Managerial strokes include shooting from the hip, following the script, and sailing with the wind.

Shooting from the Hip—The Gunslinger

Mine is perhaps the last generation that grew up idolizing that great American folk hero, the gunslinger. Fast on the draw and straight as an arrow, his world was starkly divided into right and wrong. The ultimate loner, he did the deed and rode off into the sunset.

The modern-day equivalent of such "macho" behavior is the

reactive style of management, in which folks do it themselves. They organize and compete to win. To convince these graduates of the John Wayne school of management to consider more people-oriented approaches would be like persuading Butch Cassidy to hang up his guns. They are the tough hombres and the power-oriented directors of other people's lives. They have lightning reflexes and minds of steel. Their style is most often making it in contemporary organizations. They do not typically show strong needs for affiliation. Subordinates tend to be sidekicks and faithful Indian companions—spectators who water the horses and protect the hero's flanks.

Successful gunslingers get what they want by taking direct action. To get rich, they work hard, compete hard, and organize others to accomplish tasks. They initiate and seek out confrontation (the shoot-out). They are challenged by tough tasks and work to achieve them with singleness of purpose. Their locus of control is outward, seeking trophies to hang on the wall.

Following the Script—The Superspy

If the model of a reactive manager is the gunslinger, then the proactive manager is cast in the mold of superspy; instead of Billy the Kid we have James Bond. The superspy places great emphasis on strategy, and he or she creates organization to fit the situation; Bond is the ultimate game player—adept at bridge, chess, and chemin de fer. The goal is always clear, and control is implemented through influence rather than pure power. Karate, with its emphasis on leverage, replaces street fighting and brute force. Even his weapon is small and precise, unlike the .45-caliber cannon of the gunslinger. And he often uses a silencer.

Proactive management style is based on taking goal-oriented action. It refers to those occasions when a manager acts with a clear idea of the results to be achieved. Most contemporary management models assume this behavioral style is best; management by objectives is a prime example. Yet, in spite of the flawless theoretical validity of MBO, many managers give such approaches but a passing glance. As one company president put it, "Sure we manage by objectives here. I handed them out yesterday."

Sailing with the Wind—The Adventurer

The interactive style of management is a mutation that combines the swiftness of reaction with the forethought of proaction. It is an adaptive style of behavior that focuses on general direction rather than on specific location. The role model is that of *adventurer*, exemplified by the character Travis McGee, created by John D. McDonald. McGee is a free spirit who organizes by mission and moves to protect strongly held values.

The interactive manager seeks knowledge and change. His or her locus of control is very much inward, focusing more on people than on things. Control is achieved through affiliation and relationships rather than through motives of power or achievement.

The interactive manager's objectives include not only performance but feelings and emotions. Floating within the heavy structure of organizations, such managers emphasize key values, such as quality, service, and productivity. They use their own behavior as a model to change the culture and modify norms. They employ a compass rather than a map because they don't want to be boxed in by widely held assumptions. They go beyond asking, "Where are we going?" and "How will we get there?" They want to know, "What will we be when we get there?" Depending on the culture, he or she is a wizard, a warrior, a rebel, an eccentric, or just plain crazy.

The Real World

You are the vice-president of the consumer-products division of a large pharmaceutical corporation. Over the years, the organization has lost market share, and there have been no real winners from R&D. You have assembled your staff to review the situation and seek their advice on what to do about it.

It very quickly becomes obvious that they have done their homework. They concisely define the problem as a lack of proprietary drugs, and they urge you to approve a $5 million expenditure to push 3 new products into the market within 18 months. The payoff could be huge, but so is the risk. Then the phone rings.

The president needs to discuss a recent FDA ruling that could seriously affect a major product line. You return to your staff after an hour, only to be interrupted again—this time by the corporate controller. After that, you are just able to make a lunch date with the chairman of the board.

You return to the staff meeting at about 1:00. The need for swift action is apparent, but the risk weighs heavy on your mind, and it would be nice if there were more choices. Then your secretary slips you a note: a major customer wants to discuss a large order. You never get back to the meeting.

This is real life. Managers live in a world of distractions and disruptions where time comes in bits and pieces, not chunks. It is a life of meetings, phone calls, personal visits, paperwork, and occasional forays into the far corners of the organization. Rational models of managerial behavior assume that there is a great deal of time to plan, organize, direct, and control. But there isn't. They also assume that managers can develop a wide variety of choices. But they can't. Often the best managers can hope for are reasonably well developed go–no-go decisions, and the higher they are in the organization, the truer this is. The notion of an orderly decision-making process is a myth, which is why so many gunslingers are successful and why so few superspies make it to the top.

Managers do plan, organize, direct, and control, but they do so within the confines of the game. Top managers have few, if any, options. They deal primarily with a never-ending succession of crises. The hierarchy filters out news of the small brush fires so that top managers pay attention only when there are full-blown blazes.

Management theory assumes the players start from ground zero. But they don't. Instead, they are constantly faced with end games and late-inning decisions.

The Gunslinger Dilemma

Given the above, is it any wonder that most managers are inclined to slap leather and shoot it out? The dilemma is what happens when the smoke clears. Our star is required to ride off into the sunset. Indeed, if he or she doesn't, the story takes a new twist. Once Dodge City or Dynamic Data is cleaned up, the townspeople start to get antsy about having a desperado around, and our hero becomes a villain. Even Hollywood doesn't expect us to buy a miraculous transformation from pistol packer to plow pusher or cattle puncher.

The Superspy Alternative

The emergence of secret agents as heroes reflects our changing culture as much as anything else. In Ian Fleming's books most of the action takes place in Bond's head, not in the streets of Laredo. The superspy model is evidence of a shift from an agrarian economy to an industrialized era. Indeed, in the film versions of his books, great emphasis is placed on technology and gimmicky weapons.

Proactive and reactive management styles differ primarily in terms of *awareness*. Proactive managers know where they are now, where they are going, and how they will get there. When they pick up clues that something is wrong, they are quick to check their maps. Faced with an unanticipated obstacle, however, they may lead their organization down the garden path. That is, they may not know what clues to pay attention to. Or the map may be wrong or out of scale.

The power of proactive management is that one picks one's battles. The gunslinger shoots first and asks questions later. The superspy asks lots of questions. Such managers recognize that errors in judgment are a function of poor problem definition, not of poor solutions. They manage people, not things. If need be, they will manipulate situations to fit their map. They keep their eyes out for missed targets and failures to get back on the road after a wrong turn. When there is no action, they may well get on their white horses and ride into battle—a battle they have consciously chosen to fight.

A proactive manager recognizes that there is much over which one has no control; the best one can do is anticipate developments and initiate steps to deal with their impact. Such managers know that the enemy is not the competition, not the government, and not the economy. The enemy is time. The time to do it right is the first time because there may not be a next time.

An Agent of Change

The dilemma of real-world management is that there are too few choices, not enough time, and too many filters. This is why traditional theory doesn't work in practice. The interactive management style focuses on *values* rather than goals, using a compass and a sense of direction rather than a map. Such managers know where they *don't* want to be as well as where they are going; they focus on trends rather than on landmarks. The fragments of their day become opportunities to reinforce *what* they want the organization to be as much as where they want it to be. They flow with the stream of interruptions rather than fighting it. Their very power is in *not* dealing with isolated problems.

Adventurers use a combination of reactive and proactive management styles. They react to information flow, but they proactively determine a generalized course of action. Like good poker players, they sort through a random series of events and make their moves when the time is right. They are, above all, opportunists. But unlike superspies, who wait in comfort for their next assignment, they purposely wander out into the jungle. Their mission is not to solve specific problems but to overcome the great inertia of their organizations. They try to bring about change by reshaping values.

Adventurers accept that most short-term routine will be random and chaotic. Proactive managers are careful about what they say, but interactive managers are careful about what they do. Such managers see themselves as symbols of what they are trying to achieve. In the words of Carlos Castaneda, "They are warriors who see a separate reality and seek to help others see."

Order out of Chaos

Management is a game—a very serious one in which the first order of business is to survive. Indeed, survival is perhaps the only absolute in the game. There are certainly no finite criteria of managerial achievement, which is why style is such a messy issue. The chaotic nature of management goes with the territory; it is part and parcel of dealing with unpredictable events. Since a manager's role is to achieve results, style becomes a reflection of how that person performs within the context of that unpredictability—that is, the assumptions about the game that he or she makes.

A reactive manager accepts that there will be chaos and plans, organizes, directs, and controls his or her organization to win in spite of it. A proactive manager seeks to reduce that lack of predictability—to bring order out of chaos. Interactive managers do a little of both and some of neither. In essence, they change what can be changed and leave the rest alone. Their strategy is at once pragmatic and ephemeral. Such managers flow with the unpredictable nature of the environment, and their goal is to understand it rather than fight it. At the same time, they are quick to solve a problem when one arises. The major difference between interactive and proactive management styles is that interactive managers hold far fewer assumptions about what they can control. As one interactive manager put it, "Sometimes there is not a hell of a lot you can do; you take what the game will give you."

A Sense of History

The fallacy in the popular notion that holds that one learns from history is that past events are predictive of future ones. As pointed out in Chapter 18, the real learning comes from the way in which one has dealt with a particular series of events. It is tempting to seek out a "best" management style or set of styles, but such a search is destined to fail because we cannot precisely categorize those events. How, for example, do we define the effectiveness of an organization? Can we really say that a highly productive but marginally profitable business is "better" than a cumbersome and wasteful one that lumbers along and generates pots of money for its shareholders?

Of course, one could say that the latter would make even more money if it were more productive but even that cannot be proved; sometimes the cure is worse than the disease. The beauty of bureaucracy and the appeal of military hierarchy lie in the sense of predictability that they give people. Only when the managers of such organizations begin to believe that their world is an orderly place does real trouble start.

The bottom line is that there is no real correlation between management style and results. Gunslingers, superspies, and adventurers all win some and lose some. The edge, however, goes to those who recognize their own style and pick their game accordingly. To do this, managers must be willing to prove themselves wrong on occasion, which is very difficult to do. If a manager is ever to master the future with all its uncertainty, however, he or she must be able to find out what is going wrong as well as right. A starting point is to attribute all your success to pure dumb luck. Then figure out how you got so lucky. This is the message of the final chapter of this book.

20

Winning

Never kill a singing bird.

Famous ornithologist

At a management seminar I was conducting recently, one of the participants became so exasperated with my overly simplistic homilies that he finally blurted out, "It can't be that simple." But, alas, it is a fact that management is nothing more than a few simple truths; so it is with every game until we muck it up with complex tips and techniques. The myth that success and skill are correlated persists because we need to view the world as an orderly place and because we become embarrassed to think that something was achieved mostly through dumb blind luck.

The purpose of this book has been to help managers see more clearly. It is certainly reasonable for a company to report that earnings have increased significantly over last year's as a means to push up the price of its stock. The trap, especially when last year was a bummer, is when the management of that company starts to think it did something other than fiddle with a few figures. Likewise, you are entitled to brag to your friends that your $30,000 bungalow has tripled in value as long as *you* know that the cause was inflation, not real estate acumen.

My tennis pro thinks he is imparting the wisdom of top spin, but I know that all his class offers a duffer like me is the opportunity to practice keeping the ball in play. Similarly, the winners in management will be those who put the ball back in their opponents' court last. It does not matter one whit whether they use a Western grip, an Eastern grip, or hold the racket in their teeth. Here, then, is my last rule of the game.

> *Rule 32:* The secret to winning the management game
> is not to lose.

The game of management is played on a complex layout by players who are often under stress. If there is a single consistently observable attribute of winners it is that they appear calm, cool, and collected in the middle of chaos—not because they were blessed with a particular metabolism but because they can see what is there. More importantly, they do not look for what is not there. They take what the game gives them. They see that time is both the enemy and the ally of management. It is there in equal portion for all players to use or misuse as they see fit. Here, then, is a guide to how to use it wisely.

People

Stop trying to "motivate" people; they are already motivated. If people are not performing, either it is not in their best interests to do so or they don't know how. If you accept mediocrity, you will get mediocrity. Go for excellence by finding a few talented performers, and build on them. Do not accept the stupidity that leadership is the offer of rewards or the threat of punishment. In the former case you may get your hand bitten, and in the latter you will live in a house full of victims. Instead, learn your game: know which needs it rewards and which it punishes. Then go out and find those folks who play your music.

Groups are bunches of people who stick together like white on rice. Their primary objective is to maintain an orderly existence. As a manager, they don't need your help to do so. What they do need is a sense of direction and purpose. Most groups are a unique blend of brilliant individuals and bland also-rans. Treat them all alike and you set a standard of mediocrity. Play favorites and they will gang up on you. Set standards of excellence, give them the tools to do the job, provide feedback, and then get lost. At that point, either they are competent to do the job or they aren't.

An organization is a group that can survive the loss of any one member. If it can't, it's a one-man band. Both can make beautiful music. The only difference is in terms of survival; in the latter case when the person dies, the music stops. Since organizations exist to survive, its managers would do well never to forget that staying alive is the prime directive.

Process

The central ingredient of any game is that the player faces choices. Even in games of pure chance, one has options in terms of when to play, when to quit, and how much to bet. Decision making is the process whereby one confronts risk and uncertainty. The purpose of planning is to *avoid* such confrontation. The toughest decisions are those that risk everything. In organizations, this degree of risk involves the failure to survive, and to arrive at such a decision point is to have planned poorly. The mark of a successful manager is the avoidance of such risks at all cost. Such managers know that the odds will eventually catch up with them. They are very much aware that there will be a few tough decisions that cannot be avoided and their choices had better be right—but to go out and deliberately seek them is to invite disaster. Smart gunslingers walk away from fights they can't win; successful superspies create options to avoid win-lose confrontations; and able adventurers explore the wilderness to reduce uncertainty. All, in their own way, combat risk by seeking to shorten the odds.

The problem with most management theories is that they treat decision making as an abstraction. Force-field analyses and decision trees do not really take the sweaty-palmed nature of risk taking into account. Anyone with a reasonable degree of balance can walk along a two-by-four laid on the ground. But place said plank between a pair of ten-foot ladders and you create a whole new piece of business.

Poor managers are those who take too many risks, sometimes because they are stupid but most often because they are playing with somebody else's money. As a consultant, I have found one of the most effective ploys to be what I call the "side bet." When managers are confronted with expensive decisions, I may ask them to predict the probability of success. I then suggest that we bet a serious amount of hard, cold cash on the outcome. If the managers flinch, I know the game is crooked. If they jump at it, I withdraw the offer and commend them for their skills. Faced with such a crucial decision, a manager should always ask one key question: "If I'm wrong, what will happen?" If the answer is death, dismemberment, or financial disaster, he or she should walk away from it. On the other hand, if the worst possible result is some marginal inconvenience, then the bet is worth taking. The only thing my father ever taught me about gambling was never to bet more than I could afford to lose, and the same advice applies to decision making. Make the right decisions and your organization will love, honor, and reward you regardless of your style. Make the wrong ones and even the most elegant technique will not save you.

Leadership

The primary function of leadership is to bring order out of chaos. When groups are maintaining their orderly existence, it is a greatly overrated function. Just as effective decision making involves the avoidance of risk, so the mark of effective leadership is knowing when to leave things alone. That is why gunslingers ride off into the sunset, why superspies take long vacations, and why adventurers get involved in community activities.

One of the great myths of management is that success is a

function of leadership skill; it isn't. Leadership is nothing more than a euphemism for direction and control. It is a process that can be performed in exemplary fashion and yet produce the most meager results. Indeed, given sufficient talent, a reasonable structure, and a few built-in monitoring devices, most organizations will function just fine on a day-to-day basis without great leadership.

Poor managers are those who think they have to go out every day and lead; they are wrong. More often than not, they will do more harm than good, creating chaos where none existed. Exceptional leaders are those who worry less about being a leader and more about whether the organization is sufficiently organized, directed, and controlled to achieve its objective—because achievement of objectives is the real measure of an organization's success.

Leadership is not management by objectives but management by exception. It entails leaving the polished cruisers and their splendid captains alone and tending to the scows that are taking on water or threatening mutiny. Real leadership involves rolling up one's sleeves and getting dirty. Those who constantly stand on the bridge in their dress uniforms may be a lot of things, but a leader isn't one of them.

Productivity

The dilemma of organizational productivity may be that it doesn't exist. Like a race horse, we breed it, feed it, train it, and then gripe because it doesn't run faster. We change equipment and jockeys but only grudgingly accept that we may have the wrong horse in the wrong race.

A manager who wishes to avoid failure must focus on performance, not behavior. The role of management is to achieve results. The end may not justify the means, and the means don't necessarily justify the end either. The pursuit of some magic productivity formula, be it quality circles, zero-based budgeting, or square dancing, is not just a harmless diversion but a major time waster. Time is better spent considering whether the race is worth running at any cost.

Employees will not suggest that their jobs be eliminated to cut costs unless they have guaranteed employment security. They will not exceed acceptable minimum levels of performance if it is punishing to do so. And to expect either is to attribute such poor judgment on their part as to question the legitimacy of hiring them in the first place. The paths of failure are littered with managers who have assumed that people are dumb.

Employees are getting damn tired of hearing about productivity. Bad managers are using it as another battering ram of a buzzword for knocking down subordinates about their behavior. Productivity is a measure of a manager's performance, not the workers'. Pogo was right: look in the mirror and see the enemy.

Change

Since organizations exist to survive, it behooves managers to find out how and why their organization survives. When all the philosophical gingerbread is removed, most successful organizations are fairly straightforward pieces of business that do a few sharply defined things very well. That is how they survive—in the short term. Such survival is based on the notion of continuous change—that tomorrow will evolve from today, that more is better.

But real change is discontinuous. It comes in unanticipated clumps, not in gentle trickles. Fortunately, such clumps are small until they are left to pile up and become major roadblocks. Thus, time can be a manager's ally if he or she is willing to look out for the clumps.

A hot issue right now is concern about the changing nature of the work force and the "new breed" of worker. Most traditional discussions appear to focus on how to deal with such people—that is, how to get these "wrong" thinkers to behave "right." But any biologist worth his or her salt, when confronted with a mutation, starts from a whole different premise: that change is an *adaptation* to the environment, not a reaction against it. Many managers, however, act as if employees who no longer accept traditional authority and structure do so out of spite.

The reality of work-force change is that the environment *is* changing. And the clumps of evidence are piling up at an accelerating rate. The whole shape and texture of work is going through a massive metamorphosis. The roads it will take are anybody's guess, but one thing is for sure: the interactive manager will be the first to know.

Management

The best manager I have ever known is viewed by the corporation that employs him as an odd duck. He is an ex-marine, which seems to satisfy those gunslingers who believe that their way is best. He planned and organized a dull forest-products business into a fat market share, which pleases those who worship proaction. And now he wanders in the wilderness, seeking advice and counsel from every sage and soothsayer he can find. He can plan because he knows the future is uncertain. He can organize because he is not fooled by structure. He can direct because he delegates. He can control because he leaves it alone. He can see because he closes his eyes to targets made of glass. He wins because he doesn't lose. And so can you.

The Rules
of the Game

1. People always act in their own best interest, given the facts as they know them.
2. People act to meet perceived needs.
3. People meet needs by getting rewards and avoiding punishment.
4. The primary objective of any group is to maintain its orderly existence.
5. An organization is a group that can survive the loss of any one member.
6. Organizations exist to survive.
7. A manager's role is to achieve desired results.
8. When goals and norms disagree, change the structure.
9. To gain power, act as if you have it; to lose it, act as if you don't.
10. Organizations fail when they don't know what business they are in.
11. People do not behave logically; they behave psychologically.
12. When goals are not measurable, form replaces function.
13. All goals are measurable.
14. Three into two won't go.
15. When you are winning, don't change the game.
16. When the odds are against you, change the game.
17. People rarely fail for technical reasons.

18. The secret to problem solving is defining the problem, not the solution.

19. Managers who live or die by the decisions of others are in a crooked game.

20. When in doubt, leave it alone.

21. System change must be introduced from the outside and will appear illogical and unpredictable to those within it.

22. Growth is the creation of problems, not their elimination.

23. The way to avoid crooked games is to choose not to play.

24. Feedback is the key to controlling change.

25. Competence $= \dfrac{\text{Performance} \times \text{Effort}}{\text{Value}}$

26. Need to learn $= \dfrac{\text{Value of the skill}}{\text{Cost to acquire}}$

27. Learning a skill $=$ Ability $\times$ Need

28. An ounce of screening is worth a ton of training.

29. Bad performance is caused by bad management, not by bad people.

30. Never delay decisions about people.

31. Never accept a result that is all numbers.

32. The secret to winning the management game is not to lose.

Index